MERCY
Moves
MOUNTAINS

HEART-GRIPPING STORIES OF GOD'S EXTRAORDINARY
MERCY AND GRACE TO TROUBLED YOUNG GIRLS

MERCY
Moves
MOUNTAINS

HEART-GRIPPING STORIES OF GOD'S EXTRAORDINARY
MERCY AND GRACE TO TROUBLED YOUNG GIRLS

BY

NANCY ALCORN

Harrison House
Tulsa, Oklahoma

06 05 04 03   10 9 8 7 6 5 4 3 2 1

Mercy Moves Mountains—
Heart-Gripping Stories of God's Extraordinary Mercy
and Grace to Troubled Young Girls
ISBN 1-57794-615-4
Copyright © 2000, 2003 by Mercy Ministries of America, Inc.
P.O. Box 111060
Nashville, TN 37222-1060

Published by Harrison House, Inc.
P.O. Box 35035
Tulsa, OK 74153

CONTENTS

DEDICATION

This book is dedicated to all those who are still out there feeling hopeless, alone, and desperate for help. It has been placed in your hands for a reason—it is no accident that you are reading this even now. My prayer is that you will read on—*it was written for you.* If you get the message, you will never be the same.

ACKNOWLEDGMENTS

My heartfelt thanks to all of the beautiful young women whose stories are told in the pages of this book. Thanks for giving hope to others who need to know that God's mercy can move their mountains.

A special thanks to our partners who continually give financially to make it all possible.

Last, but not least, to our awesome staff who are God's special gift to this ministry. You are the very best and I know that your rewards will be great in heaven.

FOREWORD BY DARLENE ZSCHECH

You might say that I was predisposed to be immediately inspired to read *Mercy Moves Mountains!* When Nancy Alcorn's first book, *Echoes of Mercy,* was placed in my hands, my heart immediately connected with the writer...her love for Jesus, her love for people, and her commitment to seeing the brokenhearted given a chance to live again.

I am personally so very thankful that in God's perfect plan and timing, He has brought Nancy into our lives. My own family and our church family have taken her into our hearts...our "honorary Australian"...and our love and respect for her is immense.

Be encouraged and challenged as your read on. These are stories of people like you and me; real lives; magnificent testimonies of what the power of God and the love of Jesus can do.

"The mercy of God has no boundaries,
His love for us is immeasurable
His love for the unloved is too deep to comprehend."

Let us constantly live lives that radiate the love, grace, and mercy of Jesus Christ.

Darlene Zschech
Hills Christian Life Centre
Sydney, Australia

FOREWORD BY JOYCE MEYER

Mercy Moves Mountains is a treasure chest filled with precious jewels of the Lord. These gems are young women from all kinds of backgrounds who have been permanently changed by God's love through Mercy Ministries of America.

Nancy Alcorn is the founder of Mercy Ministries. She is a woman with a vision and a purpose to see hurting young women restored to a life of dignity.

In the chapters of this book, Nancy shares the true stories of these precious young women. Stories of unwed mothers, troubled girls, homeless young women, and prostitutes who have all experienced a change of heart and healing from the pains of their past.

These stories will inspire you to fulfill the call of God on your life. You will be encouraged to help others and to change yourself. One thing is for sure, you will never forget the inspiring story of Nancy and "her girls"!

Joyce Meyer
Joyce Meyer Ministries
St. Louis, Missouri

INTRODUCTION

"You actually think you can make this work? How are you going to operate?"

The mayor of West Monroe, Louisiana, was sitting at his desk across from me, looking puzzled. I had been telling him about the home for troubled girls that I wanted to establish in his city.

"I'm sure that God sent me here to do this and that He will provide for us," I replied, hoping my enthusiasm would be contagious.

"And you think you can run your home without taking any form of government aid—no state, federal, or at least parish assistance? Without even applying for aid from the city?" The mayor appeared skeptical.

"If we take government funds, we won't have the freedom to share Christ and teach biblical principles. Unless we are able to immerse these troubled girls in the truth, we won't have a chance to effect any lasting change in their lives. I worked for the state of Tennessee for eight years and witnessed firsthand how little those programs were able to bring about any permanent changes. I know what I'm talking about."

The mayor seemed to understand my dilemma but asked, "How much will you be charging these girls to come to your home?"

"We're not going to charge them anything," I replied. "God showed me that I am to operate in the unconditional love of Christ by allowing these girls to come free of charge. In this way they will know that we really care and that we're not trying to make money off their problems."

The mayor just looked at me. Finally, he said, "I think what you want to do is a wonderful idea and I wish you well, but...."

It was obvious he did not think for one minute the ministry would get off the ground. I didn't blame him. It was all I could do to keep myself from being discouraged as I walked out of his office. *

That conversation took place between me and the mayor of West Monroe, Louisiana, in March of 1983. In March of 1998, Mercy Ministries of America marked its fifteenth anniversary with a celebration in that same city!

The day began with a highly successful walk-a-thon, chaired by 1996 Heisman Trophy winner Danny Wuerffel of the Florida Gators, then quarterback with the New Orleans Saints. Despite the rainy weather, several hundred walkers turned out to show their support for Mercy Ministries. Many members of the local news media were there to cover the story. That evening, contemporary Christian artists Point of Grace gave a concert to a packed-out civic center downtown. The air was filled with excitement as Point of Grace sang and Danny Wuerffel gave his testimony.

All of the girls who were currently in the program, from both the West Monroe home and the newest home that opened in Nashville, Tennessee, in 1996, joined the girls from Point of Grace on stage to sing the final song of the night. What an incredible moment it was to see those young women, living examples of God's love in action, singing and praising the One who had given them their lives back.

I had the opportunity to stand on the stage, in the city where it all began, and share story after story of young women whose lives had been dramatically changed. In those fifteen years, over 2,000 hurting young women had come through the doors of the homes to receive the help and healing they so desperately needed. Many of those girls and their families were in attendance that night, along with supporters and friends of the ministry, to help celebrate the miracles that God had done in so many lives as a result of Mercy Ministries.

I moved to Monroe, Louisiana, in January of 1983, following the leading of the Lord in my life. In the fall of 1982, I visited Monroe to spend time with a Christian couple I had known in Nashville. I thought I was going there for a vacation. Little did I know that God had a completely different plan than mine. During that week, God began dealing with me to move to Monroe and start a ministry outreach to troubled girls.

I went home, praying for God to give me confirmation from my pastor and other Christian leaders, and He did just that. A short time later, I moved with nothing except what I had managed to pack into my car, a thousand dollar check that had been given to me the night before at a going away party, and a vision that I firmly believed God had planted in my heart.

After eight years of working for the state of Tennessee, I knew that the secular world had no hope to offer to young women who wanted to change their lives. Time after time I saw girls leave the juvenile correctional facility after being locked up for one year, only to return immediately to the same environment from which they came.

During their stay in the facility, they would go through the motions of conforming to the program, doing just enough to get by so they could return to the streets. When they did, their former associates were waiting for them. The pimps were waiting for the girls who had been in prostitution. The drug dealers were waiting for the girls who had been involved in drugs. The gang members were waiting for the girls who had been running with gangs. Some of the girls died from drug overdoses. Some were killed in street gang fights. I watched as many of the girls passed the age of eighteen and ended up in the women's prison system. Worst of all, some of the girls left that facility feeling so hopeless that they took their own lives. My heart broke, and I began to cry out to God to show me what I could do to change these continuous tragedies.

I knew that lasting change would never result from the government's system. Having been a Christian since 1972, it was clear to me that only God's way would work. Only Jesus could bring restoration into the lives of these girls who were so desperately hurting and searching for something to fill the void they felt in their hearts.

God has not anointed the government to set the captives free. He has anointed us, those who believe in His Word and call on His name. After five years at the correctional facility and another three as a child abuse investigator, I knew it was time to begin reaching for the dream God had placed in my heart.

For some time I had been volunteering with a Teen Challenge program. Eventually they offered me a position as the director of women for their newly established residential home. My time there was spent learning, from the ground up, how to run a Christian facility for troubled young women. After two years, I believed God had prepared me for the next step.

Knowing that His plans for me included extending the program to reach unwed mothers, which was not a part of the vision of Teen Challenge, I felt it was time to establish a new outreach. I packed my things and headed for Monroe, without a job, or even clear direction about the next step. I simply knew what God had spoken to my heart. In obedience, I stepped out in faith to answer His call on my life.

The mountains that stood in my path were tremendous. It seemed no one in town believed the vision could be successful. Some of the local residents did not want girls who had been involved in gangs, who had been prostituting themselves, or who were fighting drug and alcohol addictions brought into their town. Some of them simply believed that the way I was committed to doing things was impossible.

I knew beyond a shadow of a doubt that God had instructed me on three specific points. First, I was not to take any state or federal funding. Second, I was to accept girls free of charge from all across the country. Third, I was to always give at least ten percent of the money that came into Mercy Ministries to other Christian organizations and ministries. People told me that my heart was right and I had good ideas, but that I would not be able to get the home off the ground without taking state or federal funding.

My first book, *Echoes of Mercy*, tells in detail the story of how Mercy Ministries of America came to be. As I was faithful to hold to the principles God had given me from the beginning, He was faithful to provide for the ministry's every need. A home that used to house a large family was purchased, renovated, and furnished, and girls began coming to receive the help they needed.

In an atmosphere where they were loved rather than judged, where they heard about forgiveness instead of condemnation, and where they experienced freedom in place of bondage, their lives were truly changed. It was not mere behavior modification, or simply choosing to say and do the things that the people in charge expected so they could get out of the program. This change was real change, permanent change. It was heart change, started by God and carried through by the choices of young women who no longer wanted to be the same.

Part of the vision the Lord gave me from the beginning was to have a facility that would provide unwed mothers with a practical way to choose life. However, with the home full of troubled girls and even a waiting list, there was no room for pregnant girls. I began praying and believing God for a second home that could help unwed mothers. It would be built next door to the existing building in West Monroe.

I continued to speak out against abortion at churches and events. One morning God clearly challenged me to stop speaking out against abortion unless I could provide a practical alternative for the young women who were facing unplanned pregnancies. From that day on, Mercy Ministries began accepting pregnant girls and trusting God to raise up the building—quickly.

Over the years that Mercy Ministries has been in existence, there have been incredible stories of God's provision, sometimes at the eleventh hour, but never late. Since no state or federal funding is accepted, the ministry depends on the contributions of individuals, businesses, civic groups, and churches to keep the doors open and to provide places, free of charge, to hurting young women who come seeking help.

Usually God provides through the faithfulness of many people who give what they can to support the work of the ministry, whether it is a few dollars or a few thousand. Sometimes He chooses to use one person to make a special contribution that meets a need in a way that was never expected. In the case of building our second home in West Monroe, God chose to do the latter.

In the midst of running the home and raising the funds for the second building, I was invited to speak at an evangelism conference in Las Vegas. After eight days of long hours, I boarded the plane to head home. The last man to board sat down in the seat next to me. He immediately turned to me and asked me how much money I had lost gambling in Vegas that week. Although I was exhausted and had hoped not to have to talk to anyone on the way home, I surrendered to God's obvious set-up. I shared with him that I did not gamble and why. Then I held his attention for the rest of the trip with the story of the ministry God had raised up. As we parted ways that day, he requested information and I handed him a brochure.

I did not think twice about the conversation until four weeks later when I received a phone call from him. He told me his story. He had been born to a teenage girl who had been violently raped. At five days old he was placed for adoption. He was sure that if his biological mother had not had a place to go, a place like Mercy Ministries, he would have been aborted.

This man's adoptive mother, whom he had dearly loved, had recently passed away and left him with several million dollars. As I listened in shock, he told me that he had been looking for something to do in honor of his adoptive mother and felt that God was leading him to help me build whatever it was that I was trying to build. He asked how much it would take to complete the home for unwed mothers. When I told him that $150,000 was still needed, he simply replied, "You've got it."

Many mountains were moved during the time that the homes were being raised up in Louisiana. Mountains of doubt, unbelief, and negative public opinion melted away in the face of miracles that God worked to prove that this was His ministry and His plan. Mountains of financial need disappeared time after time as God showed himself to be Jehovah Jireh, our Provider. Mountains of pain and tragedy tumbled down as Jesus came into the hearts of willing young women and healed them from every past hurt.

With the two homes firmly established in West Monroe and with the highly competent staff God had provided, I knew that it was time to step out in faith once again to expand the ministry. In 1990, after much prayer about the next location for a Mercy Ministries home, I returned to my home state and established an office in Nashville, Tennessee. Many confirmations had already occurred to signify that this was God's leading.

Over the next five years, I undertook a grueling schedule of traveling and speaking to share the vision of building a large facility debt-free for unwed mothers and troubled girls in Nashville. As I told of the lives that God had already changed, the hearts of the people were moved to give. I continued to return to West Monroe to spend time with the staff and girls in the homes and to stay personally involved in their healing process.

Finally, the dream was realized when the $2 million facility was completed in Nashville, absolutely debt-free! In November of 1995 a grand opening ceremony was held in the new home. I asked the First Lady of Tennessee, Martha Sundquist, to help me cut the ribbon, along with long-time supporter and country music star Naomi Judd. Pastor Sam Carr of Word of Life Church in Shreveport, Louisiana, the Vice President of the National Board of Trustees of Mercy Ministries, and Pastor L.H. Hardwick of Christ Church in Nashville participated in the dedication of the new home.

Contemporary Christian artists Point of Grace, who had become partners with Mercy Ministries when they first started out in Christian music, sang their song *The House That Mercy Built*, recorded specifically for the ministry. The girls and staff who were currently in the home in Louisiana traveled up for the big day and helped celebrate the expansion of the vision.

The first girl entered the home in Nashville on a snowy day in February of 1996, and a new chapter in the history of Mercy Ministries began. Since then, hundreds of girls have come into that facility to receive the same kind of help that has been offered from the beginning of the program. In 2001, the first Australian home was opened in Sydney, Australia, and on January 15, 2003, the first girls entered the second home in Queensland. A home is in the process of being opened in St. Louis, Missouri, and groundwork has been laid in other cities and countries as well, including the United Kingdom, New Zealand, Seattle, Washington, Houston, Texas, and Los Angeles, California.

From 1983, until now, the foundation of the program has not changed. It is still free of charge and focused on the power of Jesus Christ to break the bonds of any addiction, sin, or trauma that has affected the lives of young women.

More calls come in every day from girls across the country, and now around the world, who need help. Recently we received applications from women from as far away as the United Kingdom and Kenya. Even with room for twenty girls in Louisiana, a forty-bed facility in Nashville, and two homes in Australia, there is a long waiting list of desperate young women who want to experience the kind of unconditional love they have heard about. There is much more to be done. There are still many mountains to be moved.

In the chapters of this book, you will read the inspiring stories of just a few of the young women who have come through the doors of one of the Mercy Ministries homes. Some of them had been scarred by years of abuse. Some of them had chosen a path of rebellion that led them into a darkness they suddenly found themselves unable to escape. Some of them had led good lives but made one mistake that had devastating consequences.

All of them sought after God to help them and chose to come to Mercy Ministries to find the healing they needed and desired. All of them found their lives undeniably changed by the power of God. All of them came to understand that mercy moves mountains.

What are the mountains you are facing in your life? Are you overwhelmed by memories of pain from the past? Are you in bondage to something and afraid you will never escape? Are you unable to see over the obstacles that stand in your path to freedom? Let the stories of these young women, my heroes, show you how those mountains can melt away like wax in the presence of God. He will show you the same mercy that He has shown them.

Are you driven by a heart of compassion for others who feel that they no longer have the strength to overcome what stands in their way? Has God called you to carry His light to people who are dying in the darkness? Let the stories of these young women, these champions, encourage you to reach out and make a difference in the life of another. Let their stories show you how mercy triumphs over judgment. Let them show you how mercy moves mountains.

* Excerpt from *Echoes of Mercy* by Nancy Alcorn.

CHAPTER 1

MARSHA

Marsha lay in the hospital bed, listening to her newborn infant wail. She was not planning to see her, knowing that she was being placed for adoption, but she wanted to know if she was all right.

The nurses had told her what to expect since she was a severe cocaine addict and had used drugs heavily throughout her pregnancy. They said the baby would be severely underweight. Her arms and legs would jerk and she would have to go through withdrawal symptoms in the very first hours of her life. Marsha had cried, knowing her choices had hurt this innocent child.

Suddenly, she heard a nurse say that the baby weighed over six pounds. Marsha was ecstatic! Then she heard that there were no spasmodic movements or signs of withdrawal. The only thing out of the ordinary was that the baby would not stop crying.

"Bring her to me," Marsha said, sitting up.

"Are you sure?" the nurse asked. "I thought you didn't want to see her."

"Bring her to me," she repeated firmly.

They brought the baby and laid her in Marsha's arms. Almost immediately, the baby settled down and her constant crying ceased. Marsha looked down at her, amazed by her perfect features. She could not deny that an absolute miracle had taken place. God's hand had to have been on that child because there was no explanation for her survival, let alone the fact that she was beautiful and healthy.

For the first time, Marsha heard the voice of God speaking to her heart. "Marsha, this baby is not yours," she heard Him say. "I protected this baby for a reason. She is for another family. You're going to go home and take care of the baby I gave you the first time."

Proverbs 22:6 (NIV) instructs parents to *train a child in the way he should go, and when he is old he will not turn from it.* As Christians we believe that the promises of God will come true because we know that He is faithful. Sometimes, however, the fulfillment of those promises can seem to be a long time in coming.

Marsha is a woman who had been well trained in the way she should go from the time she was young. She grew up in a strong Christian family. In fact, her family attended Christ Church in Nashville, which is my home church and where the girls in the Nashville home attend. Pastor Hardwick, a man whom I highly respect as a "father in the faith," dedicated Marsha to the Lord as an infant.

As she became older, however, Marsha began making choices that led her further and further away from God and His plan for her life. In high school she skipped school to drink and smoke cigarettes with her friends. She also experimented with marijuana and discovered that she liked it.

When she was seventeen years old, she met William. Within a year they were living together. Five years later they got married. William was a musician and spent most nights playing in bars and clubs. That lifestyle gave both him and Marsha easy access to drugs and alcohol. They spent most of their time partying and drinking.

One day a friend came to Marsha's house and brought with her a new experience—cocaine. Marsha was hooked almost immediately. She loved the fact that when she was high, she did not feel the need to sleep or eat. Cocaine allowed her to stay up at the bars all night and still go to work the next day. The drug began to consume her time.

William enjoyed cocaine as much as Marsha did. Eventually, they met some friends who were freebasing and discovered they liked that as well. Every day they became trapped deeper and deeper in the world of addiction, but they were having too much fun to notice. They spent ten years in that lifestyle.

Throughout this time in Marsha's life, she and her mother had remained close. Her mother constantly prayed for her and reminded her that God loved her and was always there, waiting for her with open arms. Tragically, Marsha's mother became ill and died when Marsha was 26 years old. She was devastated. To escape the pain, she sank deeper into the world of cocaine.

When she was 28 years old, Marsha became pregnant and knew she had to quit using drugs during her pregnancy. She was successful in avoiding it for the most part, although from time to time she would take cocaine and rub it on her gums, just to feel the numbness once more. She also continued to drink throughout the pregnancy.

Marsha delivered a healthy baby girl and named her Sarah. As soon as Sarah was born, friends came by to "celebrate" with Marsha. Their gifts to her were free rocks of cocaine. She was immediately back on drugs. All day long, while William was working and Sarah slept nearby, people were at the house with Marsha freebasing and getting high. At night, she got a babysitter for Sarah and went to the clubs to party.

The addiction grew stronger and she started disappearing for two and three days at a time. She would go with William to a club where he was performing, step outside for "a few minutes," and end up leaving with friends. When she sobered up and realized what she had done, she would return home to her husband and daughter. Every time she came back, Marsha cried and begged William to forgive her, telling him that she wanted to quit and did not know what was happening to her. He loved her desperately and continued to take her back.

William and Marsha had a friend, Tony, who often partied with them. Tony had inherited a sizable fortune from a friend and was spending most of it on drugs. By this time, Marsha had sold everything in her house to buy drugs and the house itself had gone into foreclosure. She decided to leave William and Sarah behind and move in with Tony who could better support their $1500-a-day habit.

Crushed by her rejection of him and their daughter, William did everything he could to try to get Marsha back. He would even go to Tony's house and get high with them while trying to convince his wife to come home. From time to time, when she fought with Tony or when she was clean long enough to realize what she had done, she returned home. But, after two or three days, she always left again.

Finally Marsha realized that she needed help. Drugs were only covering the painful reality of her life that she could not handle and there was not enough cocaine in the world to make the pain go away. In the ten and a half months she was with Tony, they had spent a million dollars on drugs and her life was worse because of it. She finally left him and returned to her husband.

By this time, William had stopped using drugs in order to take care of Sarah. He encouraged Marsha to seek help. Marsha reached out to her cousin, Faye, who helped get her admitted into a drug rehabilitation program. Faye sometimes kept Sarah for William and she would bring the baby by to see Marsha when she had her. William was completely supportive of her. She said she truly wanted to change and they believed she was doing her best.

However, Tony was calling on a consistent basis as well and he was baiting Marsha. While they talked on the phone, he would smoke freebase cocaine so that she could hear the sound of it. He told her that he loved her and wanted her to come back to him. He described how much cocaine he had waiting for her.

When he could not talk her into leaving, Tony asked her to go outside, just so he could drive by and see her. Marsha agreed and sat at a picnic table. Just as he promised, Tony drove by. But when he did, he threw rocks of cocaine over the fence to her. Too weak to resist, Marsha picked them up and snuck them into the rehab. She constructed a crude pipe out of a soda can and hid underneath the sink to smoke. The invisible wall of her addiction had stopped her from escaping its snare once again.

Three weeks after checking in, Marsha ran away with Tony. Four days later, she had had enough and called Faye again. They begged her counselor to let her back into the rehab. One month later she called her husband and told him she wanted to come home. She promised that she was clean and would stay that way. He could keep an eye on her and she would go to meetings. Wanting to believe her, William came and picked her up.

William had bought a trailer after they lost their house and Marsha did her best to cook and clean and take care of Sarah. She attended Alcoholics Anonymous and Narcotics Anonymous meetings faithfully. One night, following an NA meeting, the friends with whom Marsha rode to the meeting stopped at a bar on the way home—not to drink, but to shoot pool. Some old friends of Marsha's were there and with barely a second thought, she left with them.

She returned after a few days but the old cycle was back in motion. While William was at work, Tony was at the trailer getting high with Marsha. At the same time, Marsha thought she might be pregnant again but did not slow down her drug abuse long enough to find out for sure.

Three months into the pregnancy, there was no denying it. Sarah was three years old by this time and Marsha could not face the realization of what her life had become. The only option she could think of was to escape. One afternoon, Marsha approached a woman across the street from their house. Although she had never spoken with this woman before, Marsha asked her to watch Sarah until her daddy came home and then she took off. She walked to the interstate and was not seen by her family again until after the baby was born.

Marsha spent the next six months living on the streets. She partied in and out of crack houses, staying up for six or seven days at a time and not eating for just as long. Her addiction controlled her and she did anything and everything she had to do to get the drugs, including things she is not proud of to this day. She was arrested twice for choices she made in pursuit of another high.

When she was about six months pregnant, Marsha was walking into a motel when the entire left side of her body became suddenly paralyzed. She fell to the sidewalk in intense pain. Someone took her to the hospital where she was admitted right away. She had experienced a mild heart attack.

Her cousin Faye came to see her in the hospital with one of my staff members, Joan. They talked to her about Mercy Ministries. It was the first time Marsha had heard about it. She was thrilled to find out that she could place her baby for adoption through us because she had already decided that was what she needed to do.

At the time, only the homes in Louisiana were operational. Faye and Joan told Marsha that she could go there, get help for her addiction in a Christian environment, and get her life back together. She filled out an application but she knew she was not ready. The physical cravings for drugs were so strong that after a few days in the hospital, she felt like going through withdrawal would kill her. All she truly wanted was another high.

Marsha left the hospital and returned to the streets. She partied right up until the moment that she went into labor, and even then she waited until the last minute before convincing a girlfriend to drive her to the hospital. There was no time for an epidural. Although she was afraid they would have her arrested for endangering her child, she told the nurse that she was hooked on cocaine.

Her daughter, who she named Kara, was born miraculously healthy. Marsha told the hospital to place her for adoption through the state, even though she had previously told us that she wanted to place her through Mercy Ministries. She knew that in order to do that, she would have to call her family. She could not face the thought of hurting them again.

Somehow Marsha's sister discovered that she was in the hospital and called her. Overjoyed to hear from her, Marsha told her that she had just given birth to a healthy little girl. Her sister told her to stay there because she was on her way over with Faye, Joan, and our lawyer. The baby was placed in foster care with Mercy Ministries while we waited for the papers to go through on the adoptive placement.

Marsha had to carry the baby outside of the hospital before she could be placed in our care. She kissed Kara on the forehead and told her that she loved her and was sorry she could not keep her. She knew this was what was supposed to happen. Then she told Faye and Joan that she was sorry and turned and walked away.

A few days later, Marsha was sitting in a motel room getting high when someone came in to tell her that there were people outside looking for her who said they had her baby. As soon as she heard those words, Marsha became sober. She had not had a bath in days and was completely embarrassed but she walked outside.

There she found a police officer, a detective, Faye, and Joan. Holding the baby was the foster mother who was caring for her. They had been driving up and down the streets for several hours in an area of town that even the police were usually afraid to go, knocking on doors looking for her.

Marsha began to weep when she saw her daughter, but could not hold her because she was so dirty. Faye told her she needed to go with them to sign the papers so the baby could go home to the adoptive couple. Marsha agreed to go and they took her to get cleaned up for her court appearance that afternoon. Once she had showered, she was able to hold the baby and feed her.

Then we discovered that the judge Marsha had to see was not going to be in her office that day. We would have to wait until the following day to get the papers signed. I was sure that if we lost sight of Marsha, she would be back on the streets before anyone knew what had happened. Not willing to risk it, we put a plan into motion.

That night just happened to coincide with a special banquet that had been scheduled months in advance for Mercy Ministries. Approximately one thousand friends and supporters would gather on our Nashville property for a formal fundraising dinner. They would be presented with the vision for the Nashville home and hear testimonies from young women living in the Louisiana home as well as graduates. I knew that Marsha needed to be there that night to hear the powerful stories of changed lives very similar to her own.

Over the phone, I told Joan to take Marsha out and buy her a new dress, get her hair fixed and her nails done. I wanted her to look good and feel good about herself. I did not want her to feel out of place. We rented a room at a local bed and breakfast, where she was able to sleep for a few hours before getting ready. She looked amazingly well in her new clothes and professionally styled hair, considering all that she had been through.

One of the first people Marsha saw that night was Pastor Hardwick. She was embarrassed and ashamed to see him, but he simply hugged her and told her how much he loved her. The most powerful moment of the night happened when a girl Marsha knew from the streets who was currently in the program stood up to tell how she had been set free from the drugs that nearly took her life.

This young woman was a mainline heroin addict. She had collapsed all of the veins in her arms. When she tried to shoot up in her ankle, she missed the vein. Infection set in and she ended up in the hospital facing the possibility of having her foot amputated. While she was in the hospital, friends of her parents saw me on a national television show sharing testimonies of girls who had been set free from drug problems. They called her parents and told them about Mercy Ministries. God was obviously at work and He miraculously healed the young woman's foot. She left the hospital and came to our Louisiana home a few days later.

Marsha sat amazed as she listened to someone who had lived on the streets with her. She could see the incredible change in her and found herself longing for the same thing. She was tired, fed up with the life she had been living, and she knew that God was calling her home. She was beginning to think that she might be ready to respond to His gentle leading.

The next morning, Marsha went to the courthouse to sign the papers. She had the opportunity to meet the adoptive couple while she was there. That was a very special moment for Marsha. They shared a few precious tear-filled moments together, the couple thanked Marsha for the gift of the beautiful baby girl, and Marsha thanked them for taking care of her baby and raising her in a Christian home.

Afterwards, Faye and Joan sat Marsha down to talk to her. I knew that she needed to come into the program and get help. I had told them to do whatever they had to do in order to get her there.

Marsha came up with every reason in the book why she could not go to Louisiana, but Faye and Joan had an answer for every one. Finally, the only excuse she had left was that she could not smoke there and she could not yet give that up. When Joan called me and told me what was standing between her and her healing, I told her to bring her cigarettes and come on! Marsha would not be allowed to smoke inside the home, but for the first few days we gave her a few "supervised smokes" outside until she was ready to stop completely. I knew God would work with her in His own time, and it was worth it to bend a rule in that situation.

All of the girls and staff from the Louisiana home had been to Nashville for the banquet. They were scheduled to leave that morning, but we had purposely delayed their departure in the hope that Marsha would go with them. Faye and Joan brought Marsha to meet the bus. She cried as she climbed aboard, wanting desperately to run away and get high but knowing that she was doing the right thing.

Marsha slept for the majority of the nine-hour drive and most of the next day after arriving at the home. When she finally woke up two days later, she discovered that she was in Louisiana. She did not remember the trip! It did not take long for her to begin feeling right at home. She was finally in a place where the Word of God was being taught to her again, the way it had been early in her life in her parents' home.

Christmas break came about a month after her arrival and Marsha was able to return home to see Sarah. The hardest thing for her about being in the program was the separation from her daughter. By this time, a divorce was in process and William had moved on with his life. He never tried to prevent Marsha from seeing Sarah, however, and she was able to spend quality time with her for the first time in a long time.

After the Christmas break, Marsha chose to return to the program, which we had strongly advised her to do. We knew that she was finally serious about getting help, but we also knew how much she wanted to be home with her daughter. Her decision was further confirmation that Marsha was on the right path.

Marsha did everything she was told, from work details to counseling sessions. She spent her time reading and listening to the tape series that her counselors assigned her. Whatever time was left over was spent begging me to graduate her and let her go home to Sarah.

Within three months, Marsha was ready to graduate. She returned to Nashville to live with her cousin Faye and got a part-time job. Sarah was living with her father, but he allowed her to stay with Marsha every weekend, from Friday evening until after church on Sunday. The damage that had been done in that relationship was slowly being repaired.

Marsha was doing well in her new life, but she was not necessarily prepared for some of the things that happened. The Bible warns us in 1 Peter 5:8 (NIV), *Be self-controlled and alert. Your enemy the devil prowls around like a roaring lion looking for someone to devour.* Satan is always on the lookout for a way to trip Christians up and keep them from fulfilling their commitment to live for Christ. In James 1:14-15 (NIV), we are reminded that *each one is tempted when, by his own evil desire, he is dragged away and enticed. Then, after desire has conceived, it gives birth to sin; and sin, when it is full-grown, gives birth to death.* Often, when we let our guard down or make poor choices that leave us open to Satan's influence in our lives, we can fall prey to his attacks.

That happened to Marsha. What started out as a simple lunch alone at a restaurant turned into ordering a glass of wine, which led to a desire for a stiffer drink. Then she decided that she wanted to see some old friends. After all, she had been praying for them to get clean while she was at Mercy, and she wanted to see what was happening in their lives. They had not changed and Marsha fell back into the old trap. She was gone for three days.

She was sitting in her car getting high with her friends when a police detective walked up and yanked the door open. He pulled her out of the car and began berating her for what she was doing to her family. Faye was with him and Marsha left her friends behind to go home once again.

When I heard that Faye had found her, I told her to bring Marsha to me at the office. Marsha was terrified to see me after what she had done, besides the fact that she was dirty and nasty from three days on the streets. When she walked in, I saw that she was wearing the Mercy Ministries T-shirt she had been given in the program. Trying to set her at ease, I laughed and asked her if she had been out witnessing. Then I hugged her and reminded her that she could not go to the places that would make it easy for the devil to trip her up again.

Several of the corporate staff were headed to a retreat in the mountains that weekend and we took Marsha with us. She slept for much of the time, exhausted from her escapade. At one point, God led all of us to pray for her and we pulled her out of bed to do so. As we did, the Holy Spirit began to minister to her in a precious way about her mother and how the loss had affected Marsha's life more than she even knew. For the first time since her death seven years earlier, Marsha felt a peace.

When we returned from that retreat, her relapse was behind us. We treated it like it had never happened and Marsha did her best to forget it. She was truly ready for the life that God desired her to lead. I asked her to begin volunteering at the office every day, just so that we could be there to surround her and help strengthen her. Marsha had to overcome the fear of being out in the world alone, and she needed to know that God had placed people in her life to support her.

Every week that she worked, I placed $200 in an account that she knew nothing about. When there was enough saved to get her established in an apartment, we got her set up on her own. I also put her on our payroll and she started working full-time in the corporate office. She worked closely with Joan, the same staff person who had been on the streets looking for her just a few months before.

When Marsha looks back at her life, she takes full responsibility for the choices she made and does not blame anyone else for her decisions.

What amazes her is how God has restored everything back to her. She does not have to hang her head but can walk with it held high, secure in her relationship with her heavenly Father.

Psalm 103 has become her favorite passage of Scripture. It reminds her of God's love and forgiveness, His mercy and grace, and His promise to renew her youth like the eagle's. Marsha's is a life that has been redeemed from the pit and her desires have been satisfied with good things.

She now has a wonderful relationship with her daughter Sarah. She and William have forgiven one another and are able to work together to parent her. Marsha's family has forgiven her and they support her in everything she does. Marsha has also been able to keep a strong, open relationship with the family who adopted her daughter Kara, and gets to see her once a year.

Marsha is still a faithful employee, working diligently for the ministry. She is always astounded at the path her life has taken, and what God has done for her and her family. His blessings have overtaken her, and she is determined to share what He has done with everyone who will listen.

CHAPTER 2

LORI

I t was only a short walk across campus, but to Lori it seemed to take an eternity. She knew what waited for her back at her dorm room. Even though she did not want to do it, she felt there was no other way. Everything she cared about had been taken away from her. There was no longer a reason for her to live.

Lori opened the door and locked it behind her. Quickly she found her bottle of migraine pills. Just one of those usually knocked her out, so the eleven that were left should do the trick. In case that was not enough to kill her, however, she also emptied her bottle of heart medication into her hand, counting out thirty pills. There was one more full bottle of those pills in her makeup bag. If she added those, she knew she would never wake up.

Lori opened her makeup bag and searched for the bottle she knew she had left in there. It had disappeared. She looked through her dorm room, in every possible place, but it was nowhere to be found. Finally, completely frustrated, Lori gave up her search, took all the pills she had and threw herself across her bed.

As she began to get sleepy, she reached for the phone and called her counselor. "I'm sorry," she said. "Tell my family I love them."

"Lori, where are you?"

"I can't tell you."

"Lori, please. What have you done? Did you hurt yourself?"

"I took some pills. Just tell my family—"

"Lori, where are you? I need you to tell me where you are right now!"

Lori began to weep. She was torn, truly believing that there was no point in living, but not wanting to die. "I'm in my room," she whispered.

It seemed like less than a minute had passed before there was pounding on the door. Fighting off the heaviness that threatened to overcome her, Lori staggered to the door and opened it to find several of the school deans, policemen, paramedics, and two friends. Lori was rushed to the hospital where her stomach was pumped.

As she lay by herself in an examining room, one of the deans entered and informed her that she had been expelled from school and would be on the first plane home in the morning. After leaving the intensive care unit she was moved to the psychiatric ward, where they made plans to commit her. After several previous experiences in psychiatric hospitals, Lori knew all the right things to say. She explained that she knew what she had done was wrong, that she really did not want to die, and that she would be home with her parents in the morning. The hospital released her.

Lori got back to her dorm room and she started packing. She tossed a few items into her makeup bag and paused, catching her breath. There, right where she knew it was supposed to be, was the bottle of heart pills that she had not been able to find earlier that afternoon. Closing her hand around them, she burst into tears. God had saved her life—again. There had to be a reason.

Lori's life was in a constant state of change, and it had been from the time she was a baby. Her parents were Christians, very active in the church, and they also took in a number of foster children. In addition to Lori's five natural siblings, there were always other kids coming and going from the house. One brother and sister had been with her family for about six years before their mother took them back. Losing them had been traumatic for the whole family.

Before Lori was born, her family had adopted a young boy. Jake had desperately needed someone. He had been in the state's custody and would likely have stayed there until the age of eighteen had there been no one to help him. Lori's mother had concerns about adopting Jake from the beginning, but she shrugged them off as her own selfishness getting in the way. She ignored the feeling and went ahead with the adoption.

When Lori was nearly three years old and Jake was eleven, he molested her. She told her parents what had happened. Devastated, they went to their pastor to seek advice on what they should do about this boy who had become a part of their family. He told them there was nothing they could do about it. They had adopted Jake and there were no options for him other than remaining in their home.

Lori's parents sat down and talked with Jake. They told him that they loved him and begged him not to do anything like that again. They told him they did not want to give him up but would have to if the abuse occurred again. It was decided that someone would always have to be in the room with him and Lori from that time forward.

A few months after that first incident, in spite of his parents' pleas, Jake began to rape Lori on a daily basis. Each night, as Lori's mother was busy preparing dinner and her brothers were playing nearby, he abused Lori. He bought her gifts to keep her quiet. She did not tell.

In the midst of Lori's abuse, her parents had a baby girl. Abby had congenital heart disease. She required most of her parents' attention and that reinforced Lori's feelings of unimportance. The attention Jake gave her, even though she knew that it was wrong, made Lori feel special. It seemed to be the only attention she received from her family at all. Lori continued to keep quiet about the abuse in spite of the pain and the shame.

Abby lived to be just eighteen months old and died four days before Lori's sixth birthday. Her death caused further grief and loss to be compounded in Lori's young life. She had already lost the foster brother and sister who had been taken back by their mother. Lori began to withdraw and close herself off emotionally, afraid of being hurt.

Jake's abuse continued every day for five years. Finally, Lori reached her breaking point one night when she was ill with strep throat and he came into her bedroom. He forced himself on her and Lori fought back. In the morning while her oldest brother stayed home from church to watch her, she told him about the abuse. Jake overheard him telling their parents and ran away.

With Jake gone from the home, Lori's parents did not know what else to do. They were devastated by what their daughter had suffered and blamed themselves harshly. Reacting out of their own guilt, they told Lori not to tell anyone what had happened to her. Lori was overwhelmed with shame. She thought she was the only person who had ever experienced something like that, and she lived in fear that someone would find out.

Jake had been taken in by another family with kids. They attended the same private Christian school that Lori attended and rumors began to fly about what had prompted his removal from her home. When Lori was in the sixth grade, a girl in her class found out about the abuse and threatened to tell everyone if Lori did not do things for her. Terrified that everyone would know, Lori came home from school crying every day.

Eventually Lori realized that she could not keep people from finding out the truth and she began to use it to her advantage. She started getting the attention she still craved by talking about the abuse, although she knew she was not supposed to tell anyone. She used her story to gain sympathy. It was how she made friends.

In junior high she developed an eating disorder. Her family had always teased her and told her that she was "built cute," but she would be fat when she became older. She hated her body and was ashamed of it. For weeks she would starve herself. When she could no longer stand not eating, she would binge and then purge. Lori felt like her entire life was spiraling out of control, and the only thing she believed she could control was her eating.

At the same time, Lori began to self-mutilate. Deep inside she believed that she had done something to deserve the abuse. Not being allowed to talk about it only assured her that it was her fault. Lori felt she deserved to be hurt. She decided to punish herself, since it seemed that no one else cared enough about her to do it. Any time she did something wrong, like talking about the abuse, she took a razor and sliced her own arms.

As a result of her increasingly erratic behavior, Lori began to see a counselor. She was cutting herself consistently and having suicidal thoughts. Several times she overdosed on pills, as both ploys for attention and cries for help. Finally, a serious suicide attempt landed her in the hospital for one month. When her insurance coverage ran out, she was forced to leave, but it was too late. Lori had discovered that manipulative tactics often succeeded in getting her the attention she craved.

There were plenty of counselors available to Lori while she was in the hospital and all of them were willing to listen to her story. They gave her the sympathy that she was seeking. She felt safe there for the first time in a very long time. Two weeks after her release, she overdosed on twenty Tylenol in an attempt to get sent back. Her father simply told her that she was stupid and that she was going to be very sick. She was, but her parents did not take her to the hospital.

As a junior in high school, Lori began experimenting with alcohol to ease her pain. The people she worked with at a restaurant drank a lot and she began drinking with them. She was also associating with a dangerous crowd at school. Lori wanted to be accepted by the kids, and to do that she knew she had to be a bad kid. She *felt* bad anyway, so in her mind there was no reason not to *be* bad. She began participating in vandalism with them. Eventually she was blamed for things she had nothing to do with. People assumed she was involved because of her reputation. Her school asked her to leave and she had to be homeschooled her junior year.

When Lori received her first car at sixteen years old, she used some of her new freedom to visit other churches. Although she was very angry with God over the events in her life and had built walls to keep Him and His love out, there was something deep inside of her that knew a relationship with Him could meet all of her needs. The summer after her junior year some friends from one of the church youth groups she had visited invited her to go with them to a camp and she accepted.

Lori had never been around worshippers like the ones she saw that week at camp. In her religious upbringing, she had experienced for herself a people who honored God with their lips, but their hearts were far from Him (Isaiah 29:13). For the first time, she was with people who worshipped God in spirit and in truth, like Jesus says we must in John 4:24. She knew that these young people meant it with their hearts and her own hardened heart was touched.

When she returned from camp, however, the cares of the world began to drown out what she had experienced, just as the weeds and thorns choked out the good seed in the parable of the sower told by Jesus in Matthew 13. She continued to drink and associate with the people who had been getting her into trouble. As the memory of camp faded, her heart retreated within the walls she had created.

One thing Lori desperately wanted was to return to her old high school. She knew she would have to be "good" in order to be allowed back. Lori had become quite adept at manipulating details and making things look favorable for her in any situation. When she met with the principal to discuss the possibility of her return, she told him all about her "life-changing" experience with God at camp that summer. Although there was some truth to the story she told, she exaggerated her own decisions and dramatized the experience for all it was worth. She was accepted back into school.

The truth about Lori's relationship with God was that the concept of an all-knowing and all-powerful God frightened her. She was intimidated by the thought that someone knew everything that she did. What was even more unbelievable to her was the possibility that somebody loved her unconditionally. Lori felt so horribly about herself that she did not want to even consider accepting someone's love. Rather than attempting to face those potentially painful realities, Lori immersed herself in deception.

Although Lori had been introduced to the one true God, she turned away from Him out of fear and a lack of understanding. She truly desired spiritual things but simply did not have enough knowledge about God to seek His plan. The Bible warns us in Hosea 4:6 that the people of God are destroyed by a lack of knowledge.

During her senior year, Lori became friends with a girl who introduced her to the New Age movement. This girl's mother saw a psychic regularly and involved the girls in that as well. Lori began dressing in all black and wearing crystals and New Age jewelry. She convinced herself that there were many ways to God, even though she knew the truth of John 14:6, which says that Jesus is the only way to the Father.

The spirit world fascinated her and she became obsessed with it, writing constantly about spirits and death. Lori became involved in astroprojection, in which she could cause her spirit to leave her body. It was a way for Lori to escape all the pain that she could not handle. She also experimented with calling her dead sister's spirit out of the grave.

Her experimentation with New Age led Lori further away from Christianity and closer to Satanism. She does not remember making a conscious decision to worship Satan, but during the times that she was most angry with God, out of rebellion, Lori would commit her life to him. When she was suicidal, Lori would pray to Satan to let her die, knowing that God would not. Later on, Lori discovered that Jake, her abuser, had been heavily involved in Satanism. It was likely his influence opened the door for her.

One afternoon, Lori lay on the couch, crying and thinking that nobody loved her. Suddenly, she heard a voice in her head saying, "I love you." Instinctively, Lori knew that the voice was not God's and she asked, "Who loves me?" "I love you," the voice replied, "and you have to kill your family and yourself."

As much as Lori had wanted to kill herself and had consistently flirted with suicide, she never wanted her family to be hurt. In fact, since her baby sister's death, Lori had been terrified that someone else in her family would die. Scared that she had done something that would bring them harm, she ran to her mother and told her that she had heard Satan talk to her. Her mother immediately took her to a friend of hers and they prayed with Lori, breaking the agreement that she had made with Satan.

Lori continued to dabble in the New Age movement, still seeking some kind of truth that would fill the emptiness she felt inside. She decided to return to the Christian camp for a second summer because she wanted to see the friends that she had made. While she was there, they talked to her about enrolling in Bible school. Lori wanted to get away from home so she decided that Bible school was as good of an option as anything else.

She struggled through her first semester, still drawn to the New Age way of thinking and not knowing how to break away from it. Then, over Christmas, her mother became ill and went into the hospital with heart trouble. Lori was terrified that she would die. Her mother had to practically force her to go back to school.

As Lori stood in line to register for her classes, she was torn between staying in school and going home to be with her mother. When she got to the front of the line, the young woman who was overseeing registration, Katherine, looked directly at her and asked, "Are you lonely?"

The way Katherine asked the question confused Lori because she sounded as if she was truly concerned. Lori recognized her as one of the staff members at the school and a praise and worship leader, but they had never actually met before. She could not understand why this woman would care about her, or how she had known exactly what Lori's real problem was. She mumbled something about missing her family and not knowing if she wanted to stay. Lori did register for her classes.

That afternoon, Lori decided to go to a meeting about being part of the worship band. She was a talented flutist and wanted to start playing again. Katherine was at the meeting and they began to talk. Lori told Katherine her life story, which she usually did just to test people right up front. Katherine did not flinch. She took Lori under her wing and became a big sister to her.

Lori admired everything about Katherine. It seemed as if she had it all—a great family, a beautiful singing voice, and lots of friends. Lori wished she could escape her own life and become Katherine. She started spending all her time with Katherine, making excuses to be in the music department when she knew she would be there and creating reasons for Katherine to spend time with her.

Lori felt the most loved when Katherine helped her sort through her problems. She wanted Katherine to pray for her and tell her what to do. Lori became convinced that something had to be wrong with her in order for her to keep Katherine's attention focused on her. She purposely blew minor incidents out of proportion so that she could have a problem to take to Katherine, believing that then she would see just how much Lori needed her. Katherine started feeling suffocated and tried to pull away. She could see that the relationship had become unhealthy, and in Lori's best interest, she tried to make things right by backing off.

Mired in her own emotions, Lori only sensed rejection. She began creating conflict and picking fights with Katherine, just to keep her attention. She wanted to fight and make up just so Katherine would hug her and Lori would have the affection that she desperately craved. Katherine continued to be her friend but sought to find a healthy balance in the relationship.

Lori chose to stay at school over the summer and began hanging out with another student who was in the same spiritual situation as Lori. The two of them fed into each other's dysfunction and things went downhill. Lori became severely depressed. She would stay in bed for days at a time with the shades drawn and the room dark. Her suicidal thoughts returned and she once again became obsessed with death.

God intervened in Lori's life at a time when she was determined to end it. She had a bottle of pills clenched in her hand and was intending to take all of them when she felt compelled to go into her closet. As soon as she walked in she found a book she had tossed in there almost a year earlier and forgotten about. The book was *Echoes of Mercy*, the story of the founding of Mercy Ministries of America. A graduate of the program had given it to Lori for a friend of hers who was hurting.

Lori sat down and read the book from start to finish. Even as she read it, she felt safe. She began to believe that there could be hope for her. After she finished the book, she went to a pay phone and called Mercy Ministries.

Although she had caught a glimpse of freedom, Lori was still very much trapped in the manipulative patterns that she had learned so well. When a staff member answered the phone, Lori threatened to kill herself if she was not allowed to speak directly to me. I instructed the staff member not to give in to her tactics and to explain to her that I had trained my staff to handle just this kind of situation. The staff member spoke with her for some time and eventually arranged to send her an application for the program.

Lori called back within a week to ask more questions about the program and to report that she was doing much better already. She had thrown out all of her New Age jewelry and music after the initial conversation. God had convicted her that it was wrong and that it was just a counterfeit of what He could offer her.

She had also gone back to the youth camp for a third summer. One morning during the conference, as she was sitting in the lounge area, a man struck up a conversation with her. Lori felt as if he could see right through her. Somehow he seemed to know exactly what her struggles were although she had told him nothing. He told her that she could be sure that if she died right then that she would go to heaven. She wanted to hear more but felt she could not admit that she had doubts about her salvation. She thought that would cause trouble for her with the school.

That evening she went to the service and realized that the man who had spoken to her in the lounge that afternoon was that night's guest speaker! She listened as he explained clearly that Jesus is the only name on earth by which men can be saved (Acts 4:12). He also said that if we confess with our mouth that Jesus is Lord and believe in our hearts that God raised him from the dead, we will be saved (Romans 10:9). Lori's heart burned within her like never before and that night she asked Jesus to be her personal Savior.

Although I truly believe that Lori's eternity was sealed that day, she had a lot of lessons to learn about living day to day as a Christian. She felt that things were instantly so much better that she did not need to come to Mercy, so she threw away her application. What Lori did not realize is that even though our spirits are saved when we accept Christ, our flesh still has a long process ahead of it to learn to submit. We encounter the constant battle between Spirit and flesh that Paul wrote about in Galatians 5:16-17 (NIV), *So I say, live by the Spirit, and you will not gratify the desires of the sinful nature. For the sinful nature desires what is contrary to the Spirit, and the Spirit what is contrary to the sinful nature. They are in conflict with each other, so that you do not do what you want.* This is not a process that happens instantly. All of us are bound to make mistakes as we make our individual journeys toward God.

Lori went to Katherine and told her she had finally made her decision and wanted to live for God. She explained that she had spent her year at Bible school hearing all the things that people said about God and wanting to believe all that they were saying, but convinced that it was not meant for her. Katherine was thrilled for her and told her how proud she was of her.

It was not long before the old insecurities resurfaced again. As the new semester began, she became nervous about Katherine's friendship. She believed that her Christianity was something that she had to do in order to continue making Katherine proud of her. The emotionally dependent behavior started again.

Katherine knew she had to put a stop to it once and for all. She had truly wanted to help Lori, but Lori was looking to her to meet all of her needs rather than trusting God. Katherine could not allow herself to be an idol in Lori's life. She went to her supervisors and asked for help in handling the situation. Together they met with Lori and told her that she could no longer spend time with Katherine.

Immediately the voices returned to Lori's head, telling her that she had to kill herself. She would never make it, she would never be okay, and she would never get over her past. Lori truly believed she did not have a choice. Telling the staff that she had to go to work, she left the office and headed for her dorm room, intent on ending her life.

Her attempt failed when God intervened once again. Instead of dying, Lori ended up back home. She called an old teacher from high school who started taking her to Bible study with her. The church really reached out to Lori, praying with her and for her almost constantly. Still, Lori was trapped in deep depression, spending days at a time in bed once again.

After ten months at home with little improvement, Lori knew she needed more help. She called Mercy Ministries to get a second application and was accepted. The program was truly her last chance. She came in with the belief that if this did not work for her, there was no hope and she would kill herself to end it all.

The first thing that Lori experienced at Mercy Ministries was love. She was hugged, encouraged, and told positive and uplifting statements about herself. Immediately we recognized leadership qualities in her and told her that God had given her special abilities that had become twisted somewhere along the way. We praised her for taking this opportunity to get things straightened out so that she could go on and use her special talents to glorify God, as He had always intended. We told her that she was special. It was the first time that Lori had not felt she needed to connive or manipulate to hear such things.

Lori felt that she could tell her counselor anything and she would still love and understand her. Her counselor showed her all the ways that Satan had lied to her. She helped Lori learn godly truths to replace those lies. Every counseling session held a revelation for Lori.

The first hope that she could get through her sexual abuse came when Lori listened to Joyce Meyer's personal testimony of overcoming her abuse. Lori realized that the key to her healing was in forgiving her abuser. Although at first this was difficult for her to accept, she came to understand that forgiving Jake was not the same thing as condoning his behavior or saying that what he had done to her was okay. It was simply a choice on her part not to hold it against him anymore and to allow God to deal with him.

When she let go of her need to make Jake pay for what he had done, the pain of the abuse left her as well. She was finally ready for God's healing touch in her mind and her emotions. Lori even came to the point where she could pray for Jake and his salvation.

Mercy Ministries was also the first place where Lori was disciplined while being loved. That helped her realize she no longer needed to punish herself. She remembers being disciplined one time by being denied the weekly trip to the mall. Wisely, Lori chose to spend that time in her bedroom reading her Bible.

She came across 1 John 1:9 (NKJV), which says, *If we confess our sins, He is faithful and just to forgive us our sins and to cleanse us of all unrighteousness*. She read a little further and found 1 John 2:2 (NIV), which says, *He* [Jesus Christ] *is the atoning sacrifice for our sins, and not only for ours but also for the sins of the whole world.* Suddenly, it was perfectly clear to Lori. She realized that she no longer had to hurt herself when she made mistakes because Jesus had already paid the price. From that moment on, Lori never self-mutilated again.

As Lori continued in her battle between Spirit and flesh, she began to realize how much of her behavior was manipulative. It was the first time that the word *manipulation* had been explained to her, and she began to see how the choices she made were often motivated by the desire to get her own way. When she tried to seek attention in unhealthy ways, she found that they no longer worked for her. She could not so easily create situations that would bring her the attention she desired. The staff at Mercy did not feel sorry for her. One staff member began shaping her hand in the letter "M" to warn Lori when she was manipulating and Lori learned to quickly shift gears.

Slowly but surely, Lori began to set healthy boundaries in her relationships. She realized that she could bring her needs for attention and affirmation to the Lord and He would meet them. Sometimes God prompted a staff member to hug Lori when she least expected it but most needed it. Other times there would be a powerful service of praise and worship that allowed her to experience the presence of God. The Lord revealed Himself to her in ways she had never known Him, and she was able to begin trusting Him more than people.

One of the new ways that Lori was able to see God was as a Father who loved her. For the first time she accepted that she was not too bad for God. She had lived for years under shame and condemnation about the abuse, but as God broke those chains off of her life, she found the freedom to receive His love.

After a little more than a year, Lori was ready to graduate from the program. She was able to see that God had given her beauty for ashes and joy for mourning, just as He promises in Isaiah 61:3. She realized that He could take the horrible abuse that she had suffered, remove the pain from her memory, and use her testimony to help communicate the grace of God to others. God had taken those things that were meant for Lori's harm and turned them into good (Genesis 45:5).

Lori left Mercy Ministries and went on to intern with another ministry in Florida. However, after two months there, Lori felt the Lord was leading her to go back home to make things right with her parents. Although she had never blamed them for what had happened, they had always blamed themselves for her suffering. She was able to speak forgiveness to them and help release them from the guilt that they were feeling.

Lori is still living at home with her parents and has been working at the same company for the last two years. One of the things Lori learned while in the program was the meaning of integrity. She knows that if she says she is going to do something, she has a responsibility to follow through and to do it with excellence. Her attitude has been rewarded with promotions and raises throughout her time at her job.

In addition to her job, Lori helps out with the youth at her church. She has gone on two missions trips with them. Consistently, Lori has seen how the Lord has used her and her testimony to minister not only to people from other countries, but also with the youth within her own church who are hurting and need someone to direct them to God. She knows firsthand that He is the only one who has the answers.

Recently I received a letter from Lori. She was excited to tell me about the healing that she had found in the area of her eating disorder. Lori thought she had dealt with the eating disorder while in the program, but in truth she had never been ready to fully give it up. This resurfaced in her life and continued to keep her in bondage after she left the program.

God brought about her healing from that in His own way and in His own time. Lori was driving in her car when she felt the Spirit of God begin speaking to her spirit so clearly.

"Lori, it is who you are in Christ that matters, not the standards that society has set. You are fearfully and wonderfully made and you were created in My image. I knit you together in your mother's womb. You are an overcomer through Christ and there is, therefore, now no condemnation for those who are in Christ Jesus." The last words Lori felt Him speak to her were so powerful: "*You* need to say no."

Throughout most of her struggle with the eating disorder, Lori had simply asked God to take away her desire to binge and purge. However, God clearly told her that it was her choice and her decision to let go of the behavior. He provided her with the affirmation that she needed to hear and then showed her that the way to walk out of the bondage was through the everyday, minute-by-minute choices that she had to make for herself. Lori wrote to tell me that she was delivered from the eating disorder that day. She has not looked back since.

Lori is planning to go back to the Bible school she previously attended and finish her degree. Although she is not sure what direction God will lead her in the future, she does know that, according to Jeremiah 29:11, He has a plan for her life that is for good, not evil, to give her a hope and a future. God has become the stabilizing force that she sought throughout her life and she knows that He is the only one who will never disappoint her.

CHAPTER 3

CAROLINE

C aroline finished brushing the horse and carefully put everything away. Sighing, she patted her horse's neck one last time and left the barn. Being with her animals seemed to be her only escape these days, the one way she could find any peace.

Her life was in turmoil. She was a new Christian, and her husband and his family were quite hostile about that. Caroline was determined to stick it out, believing that God had a plan for all of them and that she was to help them see the truth. However, it was making her day-to-day existence extremely difficult.

As she climbed in her truck she found a note written in her mother-in-law's handwriting lying on the seat. "Goodbye," it read. "Please leave me my son's baby pictures."

Caroline rolled her eyes, crumpled it, and threw it in the back of the truck. "I'm not going anywhere," she muttered under her breath.

That evening, Caroline sat in her bedroom with a friend, talking. Her eyes wandered to the nightstand beside her bed. The drawers were halfway open and Caroline noticed something she had never seen before. There was a third drawer that faced the other direction. She waited for her friend to leave and then carefully opened the drawer and removed the papers that filled it.

As she sifted through them, they did not seem to make any sense. There were notes she had written months ago and thrown away and transcripts of conversations she had had with her husband or her mother-in-law. All of the information hidden in the drawer was about her, but she could not understand why it had been kept.

Suddenly it all became clear to her. She found paperwork, already filled out, that would commit her to a mental hospital. Horrified, Caroline dropped onto her knees, sobbing.

"God!" she cried out. "What am I supposed to do?"

"I want you to run for your life," God spoke to her heart.

Thirty minutes later, there was a knock on her door. Her friend was there, driving her husband's truck. "God told me to come here with the truck," she said. "What's up?"

"I'm supposed to run for my life," Caroline said. "Help me pack. I'll explain later."

The age of the girls we work with at Mercy Ministries ranges from 13 to 28 years old. Occasionally, God directs us to make an exception. There have been times when 12-year-old pregnant girls applied and have been taken in. Other times, young women who are over the age limit have applied and God has instructed that we accept them. Caroline is one such exception.

Caroline was born in Florida, the youngest of four children. Her father was an alcoholic. He was not exactly what you might call a "mean drunk," never abusing his wife or children, but he drank a lot. The thing that was most hurtful to Caroline was that he never kept his promises. She learned early in her life to deal with disappointment.

Caroline's parents divorced when she was six years old. A few years later, she and her mother moved several states away to live with her aunt. When they moved, Caroline was a naive little girl. She had attended a Catholic school when they lived in Florida, which meant she had been sheltered from much of the real world. Now she was in a public school, which opened up a whole new world to her, and she caught on very quickly.

There was little to no contact between Caroline and her father. They talked on the phone maybe once or twice a year. Caroline's mother remarried when Caroline was in the tenth grade, and she now sees that as the best thing that could have happened to her. Without her stepfather's influence, she believes she would have truly been out of control and lost. Even with him in her life, though, Caroline got herself into a fair share of trouble.

When she was fourteen years old, Caroline spent a good deal of her time hanging out with her brother, who was three years older. He and his friends drank a lot, so Caroline started drinking as well. She partied with them and, later on, with people from the restaurant where she worked. Caroline had always loved to have fun and she found that she had the most fun when she had a few beers.

Even though Caroline went to church every Sunday with her family and she believed in God, she had never had a real relationship with Him. She lived her life as she pleased during the week and then attended church in order to deal with the guilt she felt as a result of the wrong choices she knew she was making. Her image of God was that He was out to get her, waiting to hit her with a big stick when she messed up.

After graduating from high school, Caroline lied about her age and got a job as a cocktail waitress. She began drinking heavily at that point and also began dating the owner of the restaurant where she worked. Sam was twenty years older than Caroline and she had to sneak around in order to see him. She knew her parents would not approve. Finally, she got the courage to introduce him to her mother and stepfather. They were furious and forbade Caroline to date him any longer. Instead of obeying her parents, Caroline moved in with Sam.

They lived together for four years. Caroline's parents grew to love Sam and eventually they became engaged. A wedding date was set and Caroline bought her dress. Still, in spite of how much she loved him, there was a nagging doubt in the back of her mind. The one problem she had with the whole relationship was that Sam was an atheist.

Caroline truly believed in God, and despite the fact that she knew she was living her life in opposition to His standards, it was important to her that her future husband share her beliefs. They tried to find a church where they would both be comfortable. There was one that had great teaching about unconditional love and acceptance, but Caroline still felt it was missing something. Jesus was rarely mentioned, if ever. She knew there was more to a relationship with God. Although it was painful, she decided she could not marry Sam and she packed her things and left.

While living with Sam, Caroline had pursued one of her dreams by working on a horse farm, cleaning stalls in exchange for riding lessons. She had always loved horses. After the break-up with Sam, she found a job on a horse farm halfway across the country and moved there.

Caroline decided to give college a try. She had been a good student in high school but the few times that she had enrolled in college classes she had withdrawn because she hated the pressure, the workload, and the feeling of being trapped in one place. This time she was determined to make it.

She worked hard throughout the semester, doing extremely well in her classes and enjoying them for the first time. Then, just before taking her final exams, the college discovered that she had not been completely truthful about her resident status. They billed her for the difference between in-state and out-of-state tuition, a sum of about $10,000. Humiliated and unable to pay, Caroline left the state and gave up on a college education.

She returned home, got an apartment on her own, and started a series of jobs. She worked regularly at a local horse farm and at a ranch, catering and managing events. In addition, she was hired as a stockbroker after passing the securities exam. But she hated to be indoors all the time and quit after a month. Caroline then became licensed as a travel agent, but she disliked that as well and quit after a short time. She even passed the air traffic controller exam, one of the most difficult tests, but decided that it was not what she wanted to do either.

Caroline was drinking more than ever before and her partying began to include experimenting with drugs. She tried marijuana, cocaine, and mushrooms, needing more and more to help her have fun.

She also sought solace in a string of short relationships that never filled the void in her heart.

Throughout all of this, she continued attending church faithfully, never missing a Sunday. It was as if she knew what she was seeking could only be found in a relationship with God, but there was no one to help her learn how to find it. She would party all night long on Saturday and then stumble into church, often still reeking of alcohol. There were days that she would excuse herself from the service to go outside, throw up in the bushes, and return.

Caroline found another new job, fueling jets at the airport. While working there, she was able to take flying lessons and she fell in love with it. Although her first love was horses, she knew that it would never pay enough to support her. She decided that she wanted to be a pilot. There was a school for pilots on the opposite coast, near where her parents had recently moved, and Caroline planned to go there.

Since she did not have enough money for the move, she thought she could work as a waitress for a few months to save up what she would need. She was working for a family who owned an inn and conference center. Caroline had met one of the brothers through Sam, her previous boyfriend. The very next night, after making the decision to move, Caroline met Lance, the other brother. He and Caroline looked at each other and they both knew they had just met the person they would marry.

They began dating. Lance talked to her about God like no one else ever had. That had been the one thing that Caroline had missed in her relationship with Sam, and it was what she had been searching for throughout her life. She believed she had finally found someone who loved God and who could help her understand.

Caroline knows now that what Lance introduced her to was not of God; it was deception. He took her to a psychic, and then to a channeler. All of Lance's family was involved, except for one brother, and it seemed good. The people were so nice. They talked about concepts such as light and peace and "the spirit." They even quoted Scripture from the Bible.

It is no wonder that these things seemed good. The Bible says in 1 Corinthians 11:14-15 that Satan himself masquerades as an angel of light and that his servants masquerade as servants of righteousness. In John 8:44, Jesus calls Satan the father of lies. He is unable to tell the truth because the truth is not in him. Satan's job is to deceive the people of God. To do this, he takes those things which are good and right and gifts from God, and he perverts them just enough to make his way appear true when it is false.

Little by little, Lance and his family drew Caroline in. She believed when they went to the psychic or the channeler, they were actually having a counseling session with the Holy Spirit. They were being given wisdom and insight into their lives. Maybe this was what she had been searching for her whole life.

Lance proposed to her, and she accepted. It seemed almost instantaneous that they were married. Caroline had nothing to do with the wedding plans; his mother and the family made them all. It was a storybook wedding, overlooking the lake on his family's property.

The day Caroline and Lance returned from the honeymoon, she began working on the property. Her fairy tale life quickly became a reverse Cinderella story. She worked fourteen- and sixteen-hour days, seven days a week. She had to run the kitchen and manage the front of the restaurant. The animals were her responsibility, as was much of the event scheduling and planning.

Her husband most often had his head in the clouds and he was not much help with the family business. In addition, Lance had two boys from a previous marriage who lived with them and Caroline became their primary caregiver. He would forget to pick the boys up from school and they would call Caroline to come get them.

Her husband's family held weekly meetings, run by the mother. She was a true matriarch, controlling everything that happened in her children's lives and in the family business. Caroline's life became consumed with working and caring for Lance's boys. She was losing contact with her own family and friends because of all the responsibilities she had on the property.

As time passed, Caroline began to feel more and more that something was not right. She felt as if she was walking around with her eyes and ears covered. She could not determine exactly what it was, but something was wrong. She and Lance continued to see the channeler weekly, both individually and as a couple. Caroline still managed to attend church on Sunday and sometimes her family even came with her.

After a year and a half, Caroline had planned her first days off. She was taking her horse to a horse show a few hours from town. All the arrangements were made for her responsibilities to be covered. She had intended to spend the day taking her horse to the show and getting him settled before the next day's events.

As she was leaving, her brother-in-law stopped her and told her that she could not go. There was a delivery of hay coming that afternoon, and the bay where it was to be stored had to be cleaned out. Nearly in tears Caroline went to the bay and cleaned it out by herself, loading railroad ties onto her truck one end at a time and then unloading them in a different location. It took the whole day to finish the project, and it was well after dark by the time she finished.

Determined not to let her plans be ruined, Caroline loaded up her horse and took him to the show, arriving after midnight. At the show, she ran into the only brother in Lance's family who was not involved with the business or the psychics and channelers. Caroline told him how she was feeling, and how she had become convinced that something was not right.

As she talked about some of the things that were happening, he nodded his head as if he understood every word. "That's spiritual warfare, Caroline," he told her.

"What's that?" she asked.

He explained Ephesians 6:12 (NIV) to her, which says, *For our struggle is not against flesh and blood, but against the rulers, against the authorities, against the powers of this dark world and against the spiritual forces of evil in the heavenly realms.* The next verses go on to define the armor of God that we have available to us to fight such spiritual battles. Second Corinthians 10:3-5 reminds us that we do not fight as the world does, but that we have weapons with divine power that can demolish strongholds.

Her brother-in-law also told her about a church in their area that was teaching about it, and he gave her some audiotapes on the subject as well. Caroline listened to the preacher as he taught about Satan and spiritual warfare, and it seemed like he was describing her life exactly.

Still, she was unsure. If she had been so captivated by the "spirituality" of Lance and his family, how could she be sure she was not being deceived again? She began attending the church her brother-in-law had told her about to learn more. Lance even asked to go with her once or twice. The family was beginning to worry about her.

One Sunday morning, when Lance was out of town, Caroline went to her appointment with the channeler and then she went to church. She found herself unable to sit still through the whole service. The pastor gave an invitation for anyone who had never trusted Christ as his or her personal Savior to come to the altar and pray.

As she sat in the pew, Caroline prayed fervently. "God, I know that You are real," she said. "There is something weird going on in my life. Show me. I want to know the truth." She lifted her hands up to God, a sign that she was open to whatever He would tell her, and suddenly, she knew. It was clearer than anything she had ever known in her life. It had to be God's answer to her cry. She had been deceived.

That afternoon, she picked up her husband at the airport. On the way home she told him what had happened in church. He flew into a total rage, pulling off the road and getting out of the car, yelling and screaming at her. It was a complete personality flip for this usually gentle and sweet man. Immediately, family meetings were called to deal with the situation. Caroline told them that she could never go to the channeler again because of what God had shown her. All of them turned against her.

It became a terror for Caroline to live on the property with them, but she was determined to stay. She was convinced that the Lord had plans for each of their lives, according to Jeremiah 29:11. They had been deceived. There were gifts in the family meant to glorify God that Satan had somehow twisted. It would be a long, hard battle, but Caroline was willing to fight for her family.

Caroline began attending everything that the church offered, hungry for knowledge. She learned how to pray on Sunday morning and immediately put it into action when she got home. The channelers visited the property once a month and Caroline could always feel when they were there. She learned to fast and pray before they came and nothing would happen to her or her animals.

The family was watching Caroline all the time. They became consumed with her "problem" and began to tell her she was crazy. Her mother-in-law went to church with Caroline a few times and would criticize the preacher and his teachings to anyone who would listen. She even wrote letters to the editor of the local paper about the church.

The battle became part of the daily routine for Caroline. She was constantly besieged by fear, but she fought back with the Word. She found herself quoting 1 John 4:4, *greater is he that is in you, than he that is in the world,* 2 Timothy 1:7 (NKJV), *God has not given us a spirit of fear, but of power and of love and of a sound mind,* and 1 John 4:18 (NIV), *perfect love drives out fear.* Speaking those Scriptures helped her survive the terror that she sometimes felt all around her.

She reached her breaking point on the day she found the papers that would commit her to a mental hospital. She left with what she could pack into her car and her friend's truck and moved into a friend's garage apartment. The only money she had was a pot filled with loose change.

That night she lay in bed crying. She did not understand why she had to leave with nothing when she had honestly believed that God wanted her to help show her family the truth. She felt as if God had forsaken her. As she reached over the side of her bed, her hand fell upon her dog, which she had not known was there. God spoke to her heart gently. "Just because you can't always see Me, doesn't mean I'm not there."

A few days later Caroline sat in the middle of her bed, rolling the change out of the pot she had brought with her. It was all the money she had, and she had to pay her car payment and insurance within the next few days. "God," she prayed silently, "I'll be faithful to You with this change, and You'll be faithful to me."

One hour later, she got a phone call from the art director at L.L. Bean. Some time ago, a friend had come out to her husband's property and taken some pictures of Caroline in exchange for staying there. They were made into a modeling card and L.L. Bean had received it. They wanted her to come out for a photo shoot for their new catalog.

Caroline was scheduled for about ten pictures. She spent the day singing and praying, praising God as she waited for her shots. At one point, she was sitting on a swing, waiting for her directions, when there was a sudden flurry of activity around her.

"What's going on?" she asked.

"Just sit tight," someone answered. "They've just changed their minds and you're going to be on the cover."

That modeling job paid exactly enough for Caroline to tithe and pay all of her bills, down to the penny. She was thrilled, but she knew she could not handle a career in modeling. That one day had shown her enough about the modeling lifestyle to let her know that she could quickly go downhill if she became involved. She went back to training horses.

Her experiences had left her emotionally damaged. Caroline found it difficult to trust people, and it was especially difficult to trust spiritual things because she had been so deceived. She continued going to church, but the only one she was comfortable in was an hour drive from her home. Slowly the cares of the world began to take over.

Now that she was no longer in such an extreme situation where she had to depend on God for every moment of her life, she found that she really did not know what it took to keep walking in the Spirit day to day. She did not have the necessary foundation in the Word of God to remain stable. The seeds that had been planted in her life had fallen into shallow ground. Although they had grown quickly, they had also withered quickly because they had no root (Matthew 13:3-9).

She met another horse trainer while working on the farm and they fell in love. Caroline had avoided relationships for the year she had been separated from her husband because she was afraid of being deceived again, but this man settled her fears. He was everything she had been looking for. They prayed together and he went to church with her.

However, when they went to lunch with Caroline's pastor, they butted heads. Her pastor told her that it was not wise to see him anymore. He was not the one for her. Although Caroline usually trusted her pastor's advice, she truly loved this man, and she believed that he loved God. She moved in with her boyfriend and his parents on their horse farm.

Caroline was riding every day and she was happy. She and her boyfriend leased a horse farm and opened it together. Yet Caroline felt God gently pursuing her. He was speaking to her in that still, small voice in her heart. He was telling her that He wanted to bless her, but she was in disobedience and He could not bless that. Although Caroline was uncomfortable, she was more determined to keep the relationship. She loved her boyfriend and his family and she had already experienced the heartbreak of losing a family that she loved. She did not want to go through it again.

On one particular Sunday, Caroline went to church alone. On the way home, it felt as if God was in the car with her. She very clearly heard His voice in her spirit say, "If you don't leave today, your eternity hangs in the balance."

She had been scared before, but nothing matched that feeling. She knew what she had to do. Her boyfriend and his family did not understand, but they let her go. They told her they would be there for her when she came back.

One month after Caroline left and returned to her parents' home, she discovered that she was pregnant. The baby's father was thrilled, wanting her to come back and marry him. Caroline knew that would not be God's best for her, but she was confused. She sought help from the church, but she found only judgment. People reacted to the news of her pregnancy by condemning her for deliberately choosing to sin.

Caroline was already very aware that she had made a mistake and she did not need other people to tell her that her situation was her own fault. The fact that she knew better and had still chosen to sin made it very hard for her to seek forgiveness from God on her own. She did not feel worthy to ask Him to forgive what she had done.

When the Christians she knew reacted with judgment, Caroline wanted to never go back to church again. If that was a representation of loving someone the way Jesus did, then Caroline wanted nothing to do with Him. She thought that must mean she was going to hell for sure. She decided if she was going to hell, she might as well live like it.

Slowly, over time, God began to work in Caroline's heart to show her that He would not hold her sin against her. She began to realize that Jesus was not the one judging her, just as He did not judge the woman caught in the act of adultery in John 8. Rather than condemning her, He instructed her to leave her life of sin behind by following Him. His mercy triumphed over judgment (James 2:13).

When Caroline was about three months pregnant, some friends told her about Mercy Ministries and said that they believed God wanted her to go there. "If God wants me to go there," Caroline responded, "He'll have to tell me. I'm not going."

Her initial refusal was based in fear. When she first discovered she was pregnant and went to her church, the pastor and his wife decided that they were meant to adopt Caroline's baby. She knew in her heart that adoption was not the right decision for her, but they continued to pressure her. She was wary of putting herself in another situation such as that one. Caroline needed an atmosphere of peace and unconditional love where she could discover God's will for her and her baby.

A few weeks later, Caroline changed her mind about coming to Mercy Ministries. She remembers waking up one morning while visiting the baby's father and his family, and simply knowing she was supposed to go. She filled out the application, mailed it, and within a few days was interviewed by telephone. She was told there was a waiting list.

Every application that comes into Mercy Ministries is prayed over, and the team that reviews them asks God to reveal who needs to be in the program at what time. Sometimes there are obvious emergency situations that need immediate attention, and other times God speaks to the staff to bring in a girl right away even though her circumstances do not necessarily appear urgent. Several times girls have told me that if they had not been brought in at the exact time they were, they would have had an abortion or followed through on a planned suicide attempt.

God spoke to us to bring Caroline in right away. Even though she was over the age limit at 29 years old, we felt this was the place God intended for her to come and work through the issues surrounding her pregnancy. She later told us that if she had not been accepted so soon, she most likely would have married the baby's father, against her better judgment.

It was a very difficult choice for Caroline to come into the program. She was the oldest one there. Where she had once been in charge of her own staff, she now had to submit her will to the staff in the home, some of whom were younger than she was! Still, there was an incredible sense of joy and peace about her that everyone noticed. It was obvious that God was giving her the grace to withstand the pressures of her situation.

Caroline compares her experience at Mercy Ministries to being in a "spiritual intensive care unit." Her emotions, her psyche, and her spirit were so damaged by everything that she had been through that she needed help to straighten out her picture of reality. She tells me that it felt like Jesus actually walked the halls at night and that He would wrap His arms around her and hold her when she felt most lonely. She felt safe.

Caroline's counselors provided her with all the information she needed to make a good decision about her baby, telling her that her decision was between her and God. It was not long before Caroline was convinced that she was meant to keep her baby. God even gave her the name "Issac" for the child.

Although she was sure about her decision, Caroline had no idea how to care for a child. She had never even held a baby before! Privately, she confessed that to one of the night staff. That staff member began meeting with Caroline after all the other girls had gone to bed to teach her what she needed to know about taking care of a baby, using a doll as a practice child.

Caroline was learning more than just the practical side of parenting while she stayed in the program. She was learning about the mercy and grace of God, and about His unconditional love. It was the first time that Caroline felt like she didn't have to perform, that she could just be herself. She realized that when she obeyed God and allowed Him into her life to heal her wounds, He also took care of all the other worries that seemed to constantly confront her.

One of the desires of Caroline's heart was to return home to deliver her baby. The change in her life was so evident that we felt she was ready to graduate about a month before she gave birth, and we honored her request. Her delivery, however, was not uncomplicated.

After 36 hours of hard labor and 5 hours in the pushing stage, Issac was born without a heartbeat. The midwife placed him across Caroline's stomach and she, her mother, and the two friends who were with her laid hands on him and began to pray.

"In the Name of Jesus," Caroline prayed, "I command you to life!" Issac sputtered and coughed and the midwife whisked him away. He turned out to be completely healthy! Praise God!

Caroline raised Issac on her own for a long time. When he was a baby, she started her own housecleaning business. She had learned while at Mercy Ministries to trust God to be both her husband and Issac's father. As she did that, she saw God provide for their every need. The fact that she did not have to look to Issac's natural father to provide for them freed her to let him love Issac in whatever way he chose to love him. He did not see Issac often, but the times they did have together were free from friction and anger because of Caroline's choice to forgive him and trust God.

Times were not easy for Caroline as a single mother. Although it often looked as if she had it together on the outside, there were times when she did not have food in the pantry or diapers for Issac. She continually had to decide to be obedient to God in what He asked of her. Some days she would have to choose between making the drive to church or having enough gas to get to and from work all week. God continued to faithfully provide for her.

When Issac was about two years old, I felt God leading me to offer Caroline a position at the Nashville home. I called and asked her to visit for the weekend so that we could discuss the opportunity. Caroline accepted the position of nutrition assistant, even though she said she felt unqualified for it.

Because she had been through the program herself, Caroline had a special ability to understand the emotions the girls were going through and the situations they were facing. She was often able to minister to them at a time when no other staff person could. She was also the one who knew when they were trying to get away with something, because she had tried it herself!

Caroline's position offered her the opportunity to help the girls learn about nutrition, cooking, and cleaning. She helped them learn how to become godly women who would one day be godly wives and mothers. Sometimes she felt like she was their mother, sister, and friend all wrapped up into one. The impact she had on the lives of the girls was tremendous.

Eventually, God moved her to another job apart from Mercy Ministries. We kept in touch and she often came back to visit and share her testimony with the girls. Recently, I had the opportunity to do something very special for Caroline. I felt God leading me to introduce Caroline to a good friend of mine who had been a supporter of Mercy Ministries for many years. I asked her if I could give Jim her phone number, and she agreed.

They began talking by phone, and a few weeks later, they met. Within two weeks, Jim proposed to Caroline, and she immediately accepted. Both knew it was right! I had the honor of marrying them in the new house that Jim had just bought for them. Issac has completely accepted Jim as his daddy and Jim is a wonderful father to him.

God has restored to Caroline everything that was once stolen from her. She is living in a beautiful home with a kind, loving, and attentive husband who loves God. Together, they are raising their three children to know the Lord. Her life is now more than she could ever ask, think, or imagine (Ephesians 3:20). God's goodness and mercy constantly overwhelm her.

Caroline's life has truly been changed and her gratitude spills over into the lives of the many people she touches each day. She continues to give back to Mercy Ministries, coming in as a volunteer to help with various functions. Not long ago, she and Jim came to the Nashville home for a weekend to do some painting that was needed in the kitchen. One summer afternoon, they hosted a cookout for thirty staff members from the Nashville home at their beautiful log home on the lake.

We so appreciate their hearts and the example that Caroline sets for both the girls and the staff. The girls in the program hear her story and understand that what happened in her life can happen for them, if they choose to obey God as she did even when circumstances were most difficult. Romans 2:11 says that God is not a respecter of persons, meaning that He does not show any favoritism. What He does for one, He will do for anyone who chooses to live by His Word.

God continually reminds me that the most important thing I do in every decision He sets before me is to consult Him. My job is to be sure that I am obedient to God so that His hand of blessing can remain upon this ministry. Sometimes that means doing things a little differently than I would normally choose to do them. I have often said that it is better to bend a rule than to break a girl, as long as we are led by the Spirit to make that decision. Caroline is one example of an exception that was the right choice.

CHAPTER 4

TONYA

Tonya laid in bed, too frightened to go to sleep. At just five years old, she was paralyzed by the fear that if she did fall asleep something would hurt her. She did not know why she was afraid, but the fear was very real.

It did not help that her parents were in another raging argument. Her mother was drunk, again, and she was taking out her anger on Tonya's father. Sometimes she came after him with a baseball bat. Tonight she had a vacuum cleaner and was trying to ram him with it.

Tonya could hear the voices growing louder as they got closer to her bedroom. Suddenly her door flew open as her father jumped out of the way and the vacuum slammed into the door. She sat straight up in bed and screamed, "Get out! Get out!"

Her door was quickly closed again but she could still hear the fighting. Now her mother was blaming her father for bringing Tonya into it. "Look what you made me do!" she shouted. Her father moved down the hall away from the bedroom, trying to draw his wife after him so that Tonya would not hear them anymore and so that her younger brother would not awaken.

Tonya laid down again, her heart pounding. She was furious with her mother. She just wanted all the fighting to stop. She wanted to cry but she knew she could not do that. Crying only made things worse because then everyone would know that she did not have it all together. Even at the age of five, Tonya knew that you had to keep up appearances. You had to at least make everyone think that things were okay.

As she laid there, overwhelmed with fear and anger, Tonya also began feeling ashamed. Maybe some of the things her parents fought about were her *fault. Maybe she was the one who should be punished. Her parents never really disciplined her, at least not in a way that she understood. If she needed to be punished, she was the only one who could take care of it.*

She reached over to the artificial plant by her bedside and dug out a sharp piece of metal that secured the leaves to the styrofoam inside. Holding it between her knees, she pressed them together until she felt it cut deeply into both of her legs. The pain that she felt was a release. Not only did she feel she had been sufficiently punished, but the fear was gone too. She had already hurt herself, so she did not have to fear someone else doing it to her. The worst of it was over and now she could go to sleep.

Tonya Williams is a woman of her word. When she makes up her mind to do something, she does not quit until it is done and done right. Unfortunately, for most of her life, the task she set her mind to, was to die.

For as long as she could remember, Tonya had been extremely depressed and withdrawn. Her mother was an alcoholic and a drug addict for the first fourteen years of Tonya's life. She was completely unpredictable. Tonya was always getting into trouble for doing things wrong even though she had never been taught how to do them right.

Her mother would ask her to help out with household chores, but even when Tonya followed her mother's exact instructions, she would be yelled at for not doing something correctly. If she ran the dishwasher and a glass turned over and filled with water, it was Tonya's fault. There seemed to be a standard that Tonya could never meet. She suffered verbal and physical abuse and soon began to believe the lie she was often told, "You can't do anything right."

At the age of five, Tonya began to self-mutilate. After the first time, she found she had to cut herself every night before she was able to fall asleep. When the metal pieces from the plant were dull and useless, she found other means of hurting herself. She would beat her arm or her leg against the wall, trying to break it. She only ended up bruising herself badly which added to her feelings of not being able to do anything right.

Tonya hated herself. Years later she recovered repressed memories of sexual abuse that she had suffered on an ongoing basis from the age of seven to fifteen. That abuse was the root of much of her inner pain and self-hatred. The depression steadily grew worse and the desire to die stronger.

She began to use knives or glass that she had broken to cut herself. In high school she participated in archery and purposely held her wrist incorrectly so that the bow would snap painfully against her skin time after time. Once she broke a blender in order to cut her arm by placing it along the running blade. She even attempted to hammer a nail into her own leg.

Every time Tonya made a decision to hurt herself or do something else that she knew in her heart was not right, she was overwhelmed by guilt. She had become a Christian at the age of twelve and knew her body was a temple of the Holy Spirit (1 Corinthians 6:19) and that God did not want her to treat it that way. She would cry, knowing that she did not really want to do what she was about to, but feeling there was no other way. She had made up her mind that it was what she had to do and she could not change it. Even if it was wrong, and even if she knew how much she would regret it, she believed she had to keep her word.

Throughout high school, Tonya led a double life. Everyone else saw her as a girl who had it all together. She was smart, earning good grades in school despite frequent absences each year due to the depression. At the church her family attended, she was the youth group president and actively involved in the activities there. Everything she attempted was done with perfection.

Eventually, the mask that Tonya wore with such excellence began to crack. On the outside, she functioned well, even attending college. But she lived most of the time in another world. Tonya began losing track of time, even days. People would tell her she had been in class or at work, but she could not remember it at all. Her blackouts would later be identified as multiple personality disorder.

When she was nineteen years old, Tonya developed a severe eating disorder. It started when she drove home one night past a strip of fast food restaurants. She thought about stopping to get something to eat, but decided not to because she was not hungry. She knew she was simply trying to meet some other need in her life with food.

Then she heard a voice in her head tell her that she deserved it. In her family, eating out had always been a treat. Her dad was careful with their money and they had to do something special in order to be worthy of spending money on a meal in a restaurant. Tonya had adopted that attitude for herself and even a cheap fast food dinner was a treat for her. That night, Tonya reasoned, she deserved it.

With that resolved, she began to worry that since she did not need the food, she would gain weight from it. She had been starving herself, mostly because of her intense self-hatred. At the time Tonya was 5' 10" and weighed about 110 pounds. She was 50 pounds underweight considering her height. That, however, reflected a gain from her earlier weight of 98 pounds and she was convinced that she was fat.

The thought came to her that she could eat it and throw it up and it would be just like she had never eaten at all. She pulled into a drive-through, still battling with herself. She was not hungry but she was already there. She did not want to eat, but she deserved it. At one point she had almost made up her mind to leave when she discovered that the set up of the drive-through would not allow her to pull out of the line. Now she was stuck and felt she had to order.

On the way home Tonya forced herself to eat the food. Not to eat it would have been wasteful in her mind. She imagined the reaction her father would have to her spending money on food she did not even want. As she ate, she planned in her mind to throw up the food as soon as she got home.

Even before she made it to the bathroom, Tonya was weeping. She knew what she was about to do was wrong but once again felt she had no choice. It was too late. She had already eaten the food and she had already made up her mind to throw it up. She had given her word and could not go back on it no matter how much she wanted to or how much of a failure it would make her. If she broke her word, she would be as unreliable as her mother had always been.

That day started a pattern in Tonya's life. Mostly she would starve herself. If she did eat, even if it was only a few crackers, she would immediately force herself to throw it up. For a while she continued to cry each time, still knowing that what she was doing was wrong. Eventually she became desensitized. She would simply ask God to forgive her and then stick her finger down her throat. Her conscience had become seared, just as 1 Timothy 4:2 warns.

At first she would only throw up if she gave in and ate something, which was maybe three or four times a day. Soon, though, Tonya realized that she could eat whatever she wanted and it would not affect her if she got rid of it afterwards. She started bingeing and purging, and before long it was easily fifteen times a day that she would throw up. It was automatic; all she had to do was bend over. She could go to a drive-thru, eat, pull off the road somewhere, open the car door, throw up, and then be on her way to wherever she needed to be.

Tonya also began drinking alcohol. In the beginning it was only socially and because she liked the taste of mixed drinks. Then she discovered it was a great way to escape. Previously her escape had been sleeping 18 or 20 hours a day when she was in the worst times of depression. Now alcohol served the same purpose and it was even better. It allowed her to be social if she had to be and then she could pass out.

Around that same time, Tonya started seeing a counselor for her depression. Her counselor recommended treatment by medication and referred her to a psychiatrist. The psychiatrist eventually hospitalized Tonya because of her continued suicidal thoughts. That hospitalization was the first of fifteen within the next three years.

Some of the hospitals cost Tonya's family and the insurance company $1800 a day. She went through one program seven different times. The hospitalizations were not completely futile, as each time she learned something. She was able to identify several false beliefs that she was allowing to operate in her life. The main belief upon which Tonya based her thoughts and behavior was that people who fail are unworthy of love and deserve to be punished.

While in the hospital, she was able to replace the false beliefs with positive statements and experienced some freedom. She truly believed that life would be different when she got out. After forty days she was released and discovered that life was the same. None of her circumstances had changed. She felt like a failure.

Within two weeks of being discharged from her first hospitalization, Tonya attempted suicide again. A second hospitalization of 20 days followed, but the results were the same. Every time she was released, she either became so discouraged that she attempted suicide again and was re-committed, or she re-admitted herself because she simply could not face the world.

Tonya was in and out of hospitals so often that the medical bills ran up to over $420,000. Eventually her parents' money ran out and Tonya's insurance plan expired. They could no longer afford private hospitals or programs. After the next suicide attempt, Tonya was committed to a state hospital, but they did not have a bed for her. The alternative was a bed in solitary confinement in the county jail where her meals were served through a hole in the door and she was let out for ten minutes a day to shower.

They promised she would only have to remain in solitary confinement for a few days, but it turned out to be the longest waiting period at that time for a female—24 days, three hours, and sixteen minutes. She cried for the first six days and slept for the next six. She was only allowed to see her mother a few times. They denied her request to have a pastor visit her. Finally, they allowed her mother to bring her Bible to her. It helped her survive the time.

After those traumatic three and a half weeks, she was moved into the state hospital to finish out her time. It was the first time that things were truly out of Tonya's control. Her parents could not get her out of the hospital and she could not leave when she wanted to leave. She had been court committed and had to stay.

The diagnoses that Tonya was given throughout her hospital stays cover most of the areas described in abnormal psychology textbooks. She was told she had major depression, multiple personalities, eating disorders, sleep disorders, and an anxiety disorder with panic attacks. On average, Tonya was taking fifteen pills a day to control all of the symptoms.

Still, nothing that was prescribed for her was working on the root of her problems. The doctors had nothing to offer that could fill the void in her life. She was completely miserable. Jesus tells us in Matthew 6:33 that we must first seek the kingdom of God, and then all the other things that we need in life will be added unto us. We grow frustrated and continue to feel empty when we look to the world for answers that only God can provide.

Tonya was experiencing this firsthand. No longer could she function in the world as she once had. The self-mutilation was worsening and voices in her head consistently told her to kill herself. Since her first suicide attempt at the age of twelve, Tonya had tried to end her own life a total of thirteen times. Now 24 years old, Tonya decided it was time to do something once and for all.

Even though the majority of her earlier attempts had been serious rather than attention-getting stunts, this time Tonya was determined to do it right. Recalling a story she had heard someone tell while she was in a treatment center, Tonya thought she had a surefire method this time. She carried out her lethal plan and went to sleep, confident she would never wake again.

Four hours later she awoke in intense pain, feeling like there was a train running through her head and unable to see. She forced herself out of bed and stumbled to the bathroom. Before she made it there, she threw up blood everywhere. At the time, Tonya was living in an apartment attached to the house where her parents lived. She woke them and they rushed her to the hospital.

The doctors thought there was nothing they could do because of the severity of Tonya's attempt but her mother made them try. For the eighth time in her life, Tonya's stomach was pumped. She could tell right away that the nurse did not know what she was doing. As a result of a knotted tube that the nurse tried to yank out, Tonya was left with a 5-centimeter tear in her esophagus that nearly finished the job Tonya had begun with the overdose. After surgery to repair the damage, she had a feeding tube in her intestines for several months because she could not swallow.

As Tonya lay in the hospital bed with fifteen intravenous tubes and several catheters attached to her body, she came to a new decision. She told her mother that she was not going to try to kill herself again. Her feelings had not changed; she still hated life and still wanted to die. The difference was that she had finally realized that God was not going to let her die. As angry as that made her with God, and even though she did not understand why He would not let her die, she knew her attempts to kill herself would not work.

Her medical recovery kept her out of psychological treatment for some time. When she was able to get into a center, she was told that she would be committed to a state hospital for life. She had been through every program the world had to offer and nothing had worked. There was nothing else they knew of that could help her. They told her she was hopeless.

Desperate for a different answer, Tonya sought out the only other option that she knew of at the time. She convinced her parents to drive her to a Christian clinic out of the state, about ten hours away. If God would not let her die, maybe He would give her a reason to live. It was at least worth a try, especially when the alternative was life in a state mental hospital.

Tonya told her story to the intake worker who then met with a team of people. The worker came back and told Tonya that they could not help her. The clinic would not admit her because they had nothing different than what she had already been through in the secular treatment centers.

Devastated, Tonya nearly lost all hope. In spite of all she had been through and all the anger she had built up, she still knew that the Bible was true and that it offered hope even to the most hopeless case. She knew God's promise in Jeremiah 29:11 that He has a plan for every life, a plan for good and not for evil, a plan to give us a hope and a future. Tonya could accept the doctors and psychiatrists saying there was nothing more they could do, because they did not know the Word of God. To hear a Christian center say that there was no hope shook Tonya's faith to the core.

A secular hospital where she had previously been treated agreed to readmit her. Desperately searching for alternative options, her counselor realized that there was one more setting they had not yet tried—a group home environment. She knew of a place called Mercy Ministries. Tonya agreed to give it a try, grateful for any option that would keep her from being committed for life.

Tonya completed an application and sent it in. After two months on the waiting list, she was admitted. She had a true peace about coming to Mercy Ministries, in spite of her anger. Mercy Ministries was a place that was not only free of charge and nicer than any other place she had been to before, but it was a place she believed could actually work. Tonya truly wanted to change and she knew God was her only chance.

At the time Tonya was taking fifteen different psychotropic medications daily. They included anti-depressants, anti-anxiety drugs, anti-psychotic drugs, and sleeping pills. Mercy Ministries made a special exception in her case, feeling that she was supposed to be there in spite of the fact that the seriousness of her issues would normally be considered beyond the scope of the program.

Tonya came in hungry for the Word of God. She devoured every assignment that her counselor gave her. One of the books she was given to read was Joyce Meyer's *Battlefield of the Mind*, which teaches believers that they can take authority over their thoughts. As Tonya read, she would literally hear screams inside her head. It was like a tornado in her mind as she struggled back and forth between the voice of the Holy Spirit and the torment of Satan. She had to read while sitting on her hands, holding the book open with her knees, so that she would not hurt herself.

After three weeks of intense torment, Tonya decided that she could not take it anymore. She felt trapped as if she was in just another treatment center, another institution. Although she was not, she felt as if she was locked up again. She did not want to run away from God, and she knew she was not supposed to, but she chose to leave. She simply did not think that she could handle the hard work that change would entail.

Even as she rode away, Tonya knew she had made a mistake. She was miserable during the entire drive home. Before leaving the program, she had reasoned that she could keep the same schedule that was followed at Mercy Ministries, having Bible reading and praise and worship time every morning, attending a local church, and listening to teaching tapes. She knew in her heart that it would not be enough. She decided she would go back if the staff would allow her.

When Tonya called, her counselor told her that she had been waiting to hear from her. She was back in the program just three days after she left. Surprised and humbled that she would be accepted again, Tonya determined to give it her best and fight, no matter how hard it became.

Still, the struggle was the same as it had been the first time. She was double-minded, daily and sometimes hourly going back and forth between staying and going home. Her counselor brought her to my office in the midst of one of her struggles.

I read her Proverbs 1 that talks about wisdom crying aloud in the street and the blessings she offers, but that those who mock her will be mocked as well. Then I sent Tonya upstairs with instructions to pray and seek God about whether or not she was supposed to stay. If she decided to leave, the staff would let her but Tonya would know the seriousness of her decision. She decided to stay.

Two weeks following that decision, Tonya again chose to leave. This time she had lasted for a month. She convinced herself that she would not be denying God if she left because she planned to continue to participate in the same activities that went on at the home. Conveniently, she forgot she had made that same decision the first time and it had not worked.

It became easier for Tonya to blame the staff and the program for not being able to "fix her," rather than to accept the fact that she was not yet willing to give complete control of her life over to the Lord and let Him work in her heart. She closed her mind to the truth that the staff spoke to her and even to the voice of God that challenged her. Her mind was made up and she left the program.

Mercy Ministries is a voluntary program. God clearly directed me from the beginning that it must be the girl's choice to receive help. He says in Deuteronomy 30:19 (NIV), *I have set before you life and death, blessings and curses. Now choose life.* It is almost like God gives us a quiz, and then gives the answer. He wants us to have life and blessings, but we have to choose for ourselves.

I had seen enough futility in the juvenile detention center where I worked before founding Mercy Ministries to know that girls who are forced into getting help most often only make the changes they perceive they have to make in order to get out. Those changes are not changes of the heart, but rather outward conformation to a set of rules. They do not last.

Since we at Mercy Ministries leave the choice to receive help up to each individual girl, we know that it is her desire to truly change. That is why God can impact her life so powerfully. Unfortunately, the down side of offering a choice is that sometimes girls decide that they would rather go home than face their issues and work through them in the program.

It is very difficult for the staff to hear that a girl is choosing to leave, knowing that the best place for her is in an environment where she is protected and fed the Word of God on a consistent basis. A girl's decision to leave has, more than once, left the staff in tears. It is at times like these that we cling to the truth of 1 Corinthians 3:6, which reminds us that some plant, some water, but God causes the growth. We as a staff also have a choice to make, and we have to choose to trust God to bring someone else into each girl's life to complete the work that He began.

Not long after her decision to leave, Tonya was at home alone one evening. While at Mercy Ministries, she had become interested in the television program *Touched By An Angel*, and continued to watch it after she left. The episode that night involved Monica, an angel, on assignment in a mental institution. After mistakenly being given drugs, Monica forgot who she was and nearly lost her identity forever.

Seeing the power that the drugs had over an angel caused Tonya to wonder what the medications she continued to take were doing to her. Suddenly she felt God speaking to her in her heart.

"Tonya, your identity is not a mental patient. It is not in a mental illness. It is in Me. You are My child."

From that moment on, Tonya stopped taking all her medication. Every one of the medicines was an addictive and extremely powerful drug that people have to be weaned off of under normal circumstances. Miraculously, she did not have one side effect or withdrawal symptom.

Still, the double-mindedness continued. She was drinking heavily, even while attending church and trying to be actively involved. She would go to a Wednesday night church service and to a bar afterwards. Often she would see others from the church there as well and that served as justification to Tonya for her behavior.

In the fall of that year, Tonya went with a group of friends to a Point of Grace concert. I later learned she had only agreed to go when she checked the tour schedule in the Mercy Ministries newsletter and saw that I was *not* scheduled to be there. She had no desire to face me, knowing that her life was still not right before God and not wanting to feel His conviction in her heart.

As soon as she walked in the door, Tonya ran into a staff member from Mercy who recognized her and brought her to see me. I happened to be there even though I was not speaking at the concert that night. I was thrilled to see her. I had heard about Tonya's amazing deliverance from the medication and was genuinely excited about what God was doing in her life.

Tonya was overwhelmed by the acceptance she received. She could not believe that the staff still cared about her after leaving the program twice in rebellion. She had even been rude in the process of leaving by attempting to blame everything on the staff and the program itself. As she drove home, she asked God to explain to her how we could treat her that way. He showed her that it was a real life example of unconditional love. Tonya had never experienced that before. Love had always been based on her performance, what she said or did, to whom she was related, or who she knew.

A few months later, Tonya was watching television again when she saw a Christ Church Choir concert on one of the channels. She immediately recognized the building, as it is the church the girls in the program attend for Sunday services. She also saw several staff from Mercy Ministries in the audience. Her heartstrings were tugged and she thought about coming back to the program. She missed the spiritual atmosphere of the home, the love, the prayer support, and the teaching. It was the first place she had ever felt comfortable opening up and sharing.

God reminded her then that there were people in her home church and her Bible study group who had been begging to pray for her but she had been closed to it. She did not trust other people to pray for her yet. As God brought back memories of her time at Mercy Ministries and the victories she had experienced there as a result of opening her heart, Tonya realized that she would have to take a risk once again. She would have to trust the people He had put in her life then, away from Mercy Ministries, to pray for her. She let down her walls and God was able to do an amazing, transforming work in her life.

Mercy Ministries had planted seeds in Tonya that had gone deep into her heart. She recommitted herself to the practice of daily Bible reading and praise and worship, as well as listening to teaching tapes to help her grow. As she became involved in her local church, they helped her begin living what she was learning. She was becoming a doer of the Word, and not just a hearer (James 1:22).

It was during a New Year's Eve service with the college group of her church that God convicted her of her double-mindedness.

"Choose you this day who you are going to serve," He spoke to her heart. "Either come with Me or stay and play in the world." Tonya chose God, just as Joshua did when he gave the same direction to the people of Israel in Joshua 24:15. He declared, *as for me and my house, we will serve the Lord.* That night she made the decision to be radically obedient to Him. Her mind was finally made up in the right way. She was completely dedicated to God, once and for all.

Miracles began falling into place in Tonya's life. Because she had withdrawn so many times from college, she had defaulted on her loans. She wanted to go back to school, but because of the loans and the fact that her psychiatrist had declared her permanently mentally disabled, it seemed impossible.

The one chance she had was for her psychiatrist to write a letter giving her permission to go back to school. When Tonya was finally able to get an appointment, she boldly told the psychiatrist how God had delivered her and set her free. He asked her about the voices and she told him that they were demonic influences over which she now had authority (2 Corinthians 10:5). He asked her about self-mutilation and she declared that she no longer had to do that because the Blood of Jesus had paid the penalty for her (Revelation 1:5). He told her that when the depression came back, she could come see him again. She told him that she no longer put her hope in circumstances but in Jesus Christ, who is the same yesterday, today, and forever (Hebrews 13:8), so she would not need to see him again.

Finally he threw up his hands, labeled her with a temporary religious fixation, which he was sure would eventually go away, and wrote a letter stating that she could return to school! It was a perfect example of 1 Corinthians 1:19, where God says He will destroy the wisdom of the wise and frustrate the intelligence of the intelligent. The fact that the psychiatrist had originally declared her permanently mentally disabled meant that all $8,000 of her previous school loans were forgiven, and nothing remained to keep Tonya from pursuing her education.

Tonya kept in touch with us and we were thrilled to hear about her progress. I invited her to come to Nashville and give her testimony at Christ Church on a day when I had been asked to share the vision of Mercy Ministries with their congregation of 5,000. As I stood with her on the platform and listened to her share her story, I felt God speaking to my heart. "Wouldn't she make a great counselor?"

Tonya graduated in December of 1998 with a degree in psychology. Throughout her schooling, she used every opportunity she had to present the Gospel. Whenever she gave an oral report, she found a way to weave in her testimony. Without fail, you could hear a pin drop in the room every time. It was so powerful for her to stand up in front of her class, describe a clinical disorder and the secular treatments for it, and then explain that she herself had once been diagnosed with that very same disorder and the only thing that had worked for her was the power of God setting her free!

After graduation, Tonya began working for Mercy Ministries as a counselor in one of our homes. She is great with the girls, sharing her testimony and encouraging them that if she can make it, so can they.

One of Tonya's talents is artwork, and she volunteered to paint a mural on the wall of her brother's newborn baby's nursery. It just happened that her brother was a football player for the New England Patriots at the time, and soon the entire team knew about Tonya's artistic talents. Many requests for murals to be painted in different homes started pouring in from other members of her brother's team, and out of this demand, a prosperous business grew! Later that same year, the New England Patriots went to the Superbowl, and her brother played on the championship team. He rode in the victory parade and chose his sister Tonya to ride with him. This girl, who had once been sentenced to a life in an institution, was now riding in a car of a victory parade!

Tonya consistently spreads the word about the changes God has done in her life. She is not ashamed to share her past, and enthusiastically tells how God brought her from darkness to light. In fact, she still shares her story with the girls in our program and in the community, and is an encouragement and example that God can and will put a broken life back together.

She is a woman of her word. When she makes up her mind to do something, she does not quit until it is done and done right. Fortunately, today what she has set her mind to do is to tell the world about the transforming power of God that has worked miracles in her life, and how it can set all of us free if we will surrender to Him.

CHAPTER 5

VENUS

Venus sat still, the words the doctor had just spoken reverberating inside her head. "You're pregnant."

A thousand thoughts ran through her brain at one time. Having a baby now would ruin her life. She had already dropped out of college because she had been so sick. She would lose everything.

Everyone would be mad at her. She was too embarrassed to tell her family. They would say that she was just like her mother and everything they used to say about her would be true. She would not make it. She would end up just like all the rest of them. She would be trapped.

She thought an abortion must be the only solution. No one had to know. Venus could handle this by herself. She was in control of her own destiny, just like she had always said she would be.

Her boyfriend was far from supportive, but at least he was willing to pay for half of the abortion. They told everyone they were going out of town for the weekend and left the state. Everything went wrong on the trip—the keys got locked in the car, the hotel did not have a reservation for them, George forgot his half of the money. Venus knew she should not be doing this and apparently someone was trying to tell her the same thing. But she had already made up her mind. As far as she knew there was no other choice.

She lay on the table, alone and terrified. George had dropped her off hours ago, telling her to call him when it was over. The nurse did an ultrasound to pinpoint the location of the baby. Venus turned her head so she would not have to look at the screen.

"Oh," she heard the nurse say. "There are two."

"Two?" Venus repeated in disbelief. "Twins?"

"It's no problem," the nurse assured her quickly. "No problem at all."

There was no comfort in her words. Everything within Venus wanted to get up and run from the clinic, but she could not. She did not think there was anywhere to go.

Venus fought back tears, not wanting to let the nurse see her cry. The doctor came in. With barely a word to her he performed the abortion. Venus gripped the nurse's hand and squeezed her eyes shut until he finished.

"Are you sure you got them?" she whispered, losing the battle with her tears.

He looked down into the basin he held in his hands. "Yep," he replied brusquely. "Both of them."

Immediately waves of guilt and regret washed over Venus. The nurse left her alone to get dressed but she simply lay there and cried.

The circumstances in which Venus grew up were far from ideal. She was the oldest of three children born to a single mother, Gwen, who had Venus when she was just eighteen years old. Gwen's mother had been a single mother herself and had been shot and killed when Gwen was just a child. She and her five siblings grew up without their mother or father.

Gwen's great-aunt and her husband adopted them when their mother was killed. All their children were grown, and even though several of the kids were now having kids of their own, they still lived in the same house. The house was crowded and tense with so many people living there.

Venus and her cousins knew her mother's adoptive parents as Grandma and Grandpa. Her grandfather was a raging alcoholic who often flew into screaming fits that included throwing and breaking things. While he was not physically abusive to the children or grandchildren, his unpredictability frightened them. Everyone felt that they had to walk on eggshells around him.

His behavior was not the only thing that caused tension in the house. Arguments between the brothers and sisters were common and often heated. Eventually the stress level became so high that Venus's grandparents moved out and left the house to the children.

At six years old, Venus became the caretaker for her four-year-old brother and one-year-old sister. Gwen worked long hours at two jobs to provide for them. She went above and beyond to be sure that her children had what they needed and wanted. Venus never really knew that she was poor because her mother spoiled her and her brother and sister as much as possible.

It was about this time that Gwen met and started dating the man who would later become her husband. Venus did not get along with her future stepfather from the beginning. Victor moved into the already full house very soon after he began dating Gwen. Since Venus was in charge of her brother and sister, she felt he was taking over her turf when he began to instruct and discipline them. She especially did not like being told what to do.

The hostility between them only worsened with time. He seemed to single Venus out, perhaps because she was the oldest and most vocal. More of his verbal and emotional abuse was directed towards her, and his punishment methods were violent and mean. He spanked Venus with car radiator belts and once tried to strangle her when a fight got out of hand. Victor often lied and told Gwen that Venus was doing things that she was not, just so he would have an excuse to punish her.

After about a year and a half, Gwen and Victor and the kids moved out of the house. Six months later Gwen and Victor married. As Venus watched Victor treat her mother badly, she lost respect for Gwen. She thought her mother was weak because she did not stand up to her husband when he said he did not love her or that he was ashamed of her. Venus became angry when Victor stayed out all night, returned home drunk, and her mother remained silent. She was furious when her mother stood by and did nothing while Victor physically abused Venus.

The relationship between Venus and her mother was distant at best. The daily example of Gwen and Victor's relationship gave Venus warped ideas about marriage and the values of men and women. She decided that no man would ever tell her what to do. Venus would be the master of her own destiny.

She was so miserable at home that she began looking for ways to stay out of the house, even when she was just in elementary school. Every summer she went to stay with her aunt and helped her raise her five children. During the school year she looked for activities that would keep her away from home. Whenever she found something to get involved in, her stepfather always made her quit. She was not even allowed to have friends.

If she just talked to a boy and Victor found out about it, he would accuse her of being sexually active with him. He lied to Gwen, saying that he had caught them together, and she believed him. No matter how hard Venus tried to do something else, it always seemed to end up that she would come home from school and watch television all afternoon. The whole time she would listen to her mother and stepfather rant and rave about how they wanted the kids out of the house. She felt trapped.

Venus always had difficulty with her schoolwork. Her mother had dropped out of high school and used that as an excuse for why many things in her life were the way they were. Although Venus was determined in her heart to be different, she struggled in school. There was no one to encourage or help her. Her stepfather only put her down for her lack of achievement, telling her that she was stupid and would never amount to anything.

Venus seemed to experience rejection from her whole family. She was teased constantly because she had a different father than her brother and sister. Her birthfather had been around when she was a little girl, but he and her stepfather had fought so much that he stopped coming to see her. She thought it was her fault and that he must have stopped loving her.

Her younger brother, Darryl, was born with a heart murmur. The doctors said that he would not live beyond the age of six so he received all of the attention in the family and was never disciplined. He got away with everything. Gwen told Venus straight out that she loved Darryl the best. Venus felt rejected again.

Eventually Gwen stopped paying any attention to her children. The abuse she suffered from her husband slowly drained the life from her. Venus watched as her mother seemed to emotionally die. She wanted to be alone most of the time and would lock the children outside to play or lock herself in the bedroom and watch television all day. Venus almost completely lost her mother and that was one more rejection in her life.

As Venus grew older she continued to look for ways to stay away from home. In the eighth grade she moved in with her aunt and uncle, but things did not work out. They had a house full of stepchildren and their own children and Venus never felt she fit in. Her cousins teased her unmercifully, damaging her emotions even further. She returned home after about a year.

In high school she was painfully shy. Terrified of rejection, she withdrew far within herself so that no one could know who she was. Venus thought she was fat, dumb, and ugly. Her family had always told her that she was and she had no reason to believe otherwise. She lived in paralyzing fear that someone would say something to her that would hurt her feelings. She avoided everyone.

Venus moved out of state to live with her cousin for her junior year in high school. By this time, Venus had a lot of ideas about how she wanted things to be. She was fed up with the life she had been living and determined things would change. There was a great deal of anger built up inside of her towards her mother and the way she had allowed her to grow up. She wanted to go to college and make something of herself. Most of all, she was never going to let any man tell her what to do.

When she began dating, Venus was the one who set the limits on physical contact. She wanted to be a good girl. While she was living with her cousin, however, a boy Venus was friends with would not stop when she asked him to stop. He forced himself on her. That was the way she lost her virginity. The experience crushed her and made her realize she did not have as much control as she wanted to think she had.

Her attitude towards men spilled over into her attitude towards God. For most of her life, Venus had gone to church with a lady who came to their house and picked them up every Sunday. She did not understand everything she heard, but there was something that drew her towards a relationship with God. Venus had asked to be baptized at six years old, believing in her child-like way that it was simply the right thing to do. Now, however, she was becoming a woman who wanted to make her own decisions and control her own life. If she was not going to let any man tell her what to do, she certainly was not going to let God tell her what to do.

At the end of that school year, her stepfather made her come home. Life at home had not improved. It had become even worse. Her younger brother, Darryl, had become quite aggressive and belligerent. He controlled the family. Darryl started picking fights with Venus, egging her on to say something that would give him an excuse to beat her up. Every time they fought and Venus ended up hurt, her mother told her that it was her fault. She was better off staying quiet.

A few months later her aunt's husband died and Venus moved in to help take care of the kids. She was relieved to have an escape from her brother's torment. During that time, her aunt sat her down to have a heart-to-heart talk. She wanted Venus to give her permission to start dating again. At first Venus did not understand why her aunt felt she had to ask her for permission—until she realized that the man her aunt wanted to date was Venus' birthfather.

Her aunt calmly explained to Venus that they had dated for a long time when they were younger. He had cared deeply for her but she used him. When her aunt broke up with him, he started dating Gwen. Venus was the product of that relationship. That, her aunt said, made Venus a rebound baby. Now that both her aunt and her father were single again, they wanted to get back together. Venus told her aunt that it was fine if they wanted to date. She never told her how much it hurt knowing that she was a rebound baby. It dumped more rejection onto the already overflowing heap.

Venus managed to graduate high school with a C average. Firmly believing that going to college was the only thing she could do to make a decent life for herself, she applied and was accepted to a state school in her hometown. She had to beg her mother for eight dollars in order to pay the application fee for a grant that would cover her tuition and books. Her entire family was unsupportive of her, but she was determined to make it on her own.

Although school continued to be difficult for Venus, she struggled her way through the classes. She continued living at home but got a job so she would not have to remain completely dependent on her mother. By the time she was a sophomore, she was supporting her younger sister as well as herself. Her mother was giving all of her money to her husband and son and there was none left to care for either of the girls.

It was during her sophomore year that she met George. He had a girlfriend and a baby and Venus was not interested at first. But he kept calling her. After he broke up with his girlfriend, he and Venus began dating. She became quickly entangled in the web of his life and it was difficult to break free.

When she found herself pregnant, she thought an abortion was the only answer. As soon as it was over, she knew it was the worst decision she had ever made. Venus believed she had committed a sin that God could never forgive. From that point on, Venus did not think what she did mattered. There was nothing worse than what she had already done.

George dumped her and went back to his old girlfriend the night they returned from having the abortion. Stunned and humiliated, Venus felt the old pain of rejection begin to take over once again. After another violent fight with her brother, she moved into her grandmother's house to get away but returned after a month.

While staying with her grandmother Venus became reacquainted with a man she had known for most of her life. Adam was considerably older than Venus. He knew all the right things to say and promised Venus everything she wanted. He even told her that if she moved in with him, he would set her up with a car and she could go back to school. That was the one thing Venus wanted more than anything and he knew it.

Venus did not love Adam; she barely even liked him. However, she saw him as an escape. Anything was better than living at home with her family. She thought if she lived with him for six months, she could save up enough money to get out on her own. She knew she was just using him but did not care.

At first Adam kept his promises. Venus was able to go back to school and he drove her there and back. She soon noticed that he was becoming more and more controlling. He always wanted to know where she was and what she was doing. Still, Venus did not complain. She had made the choice to live with him and was willing to put up with the consequences. It was what she believed she had to do to get what she wanted.

Slowly Adam began to take everything away from Venus. He told her that her family was against them and she was not to talk to them anymore. He stopped taking her to school when he found her talking with a guy on campus. Soon he was telling her what to wear, how to fix her hair, and what friends she could and could not see. His jealous rages often sparked physical fights that Venus always lost.

It was not long before Venus realized that she was trapped in the exact life she had sworn she would never have. Adam was making all of her decisions for her. It had been her choice to move in with him so there was no one else to blame. In spite of her dreams and ideals, her experience had taught her that this was the way life was. It was what she expected. There seemed to be nothing she could do about it.

Venus became a prisoner in Adam's home. He monitored everything she did. She never left the house unless he was with her. She did little more than sleep and watch television. He kept no food in the house so she only ate when he brought her something, which he did sporadically. Depressed, angry, and disappointed with her life, she felt betrayed. She thought even God must have deserted her.

Fights with Adam were not frequent, but they were violent. Mostly he used tactics of fear and intimidation to keep her under his control. He told her it was his destiny to kill her. Once, he took her to the library to find a newspaper article about her grandmother's murder. He told her he was going to copy it and have it framed so that he could use it to remind Venus what would happen to her if she ever tried to leave. He constantly threatened her with a shotgun. Twice he fired it at her, missing narrowly.

The torture went on for four years. By the last year, Venus was convinced that he would kill her. She was losing hope for any kind of escape. She had tried to leave twice and both times he had found her and severely beat her. She thought about killing herself but did not want to give him the satisfaction of knowing that he had pushed her to that extreme.

While she waited to die, she began to turn back to God. She had grown up knowing about Him, and as she contemplated death, she wanted to know for sure that she would be with Him. She started reading her Bible again. Alone in the house, she prayed, had praise and worship by herself in her living room, and wrote letters to television evangelists. They were her only source of encouragement. It occurred to her that if she wanted to survive Adam's abuse, only God could help her.

Venus began asking God for a miracle and praying for a way out. It came one day in a most unexpected form—her family. Her sister and cousin stopped by to see her but Adam told them she was not home. He cursed them and sent them away. After they were gone, he took off. As Venus was looking out the window, she saw her sister and cousin drive by again.

Quickly she flashed the lights to let them know that she was inside the house. They stopped and she ran out to the street, finally agreeing to leave with them.

"If you want to go, you have to go right now," they told her. "You can't take anything with you."

"Just wait one minute," she pleaded. "I have to get something." Hurrying inside, Venus grabbed her Bible and a notebook filled with poems she had been writing. She left with nothing else except the clothes on her back.

Her aunt bought her a bus ticket to a city where a friend of hers lived. When she arrived, Venus discovered that this friend thought the best thing would be for Venus to stay in a homeless shelter. Although she was not thrilled with the circumstances, she was glad to be away from Adam. She decided to make the best of it.

Immediately she began trying to get a job but became very ill. The rules of the shelter stated that you had to be out by eight o'clock in the morning so she had no choice but to leave. She continued to look for work. Soon she was too sick to even do that and someone at the shelter got her a doctor's appointment. Her worst fears were confirmed—she was pregnant.

The nurse told her that the state would pay for her to have an abortion since she was living in a homeless shelter. Venus did not even think twice about the offer. After her first experience, she could never go through that again. Right away she knew that she would place this baby for adoption. She began making calls to find an agency that would help her make the arrangements.

Because she was so sick during her pregnancy, she was unable to stay at the homeless shelter. A counselor there told her about Mercy Ministries and Venus filled out an application and sent it in. Not entirely convinced that she wanted to come, she continued looking for a job. Part of her was still determined that she could make it on her own in spite of her circumstances.

She moved around to several different shelters for about two months. She grew frustrated with her lack of progress and called Mercy Ministries again. A time for her telephone interview was set. When the time arrived, Venus realized that she had just enough money to either take the bus back home, get something to eat, or make the call from a pay phone. She decided to call.

Within a few days, Venus was in the program. From the first moment she walked through the door, she was amazed. When she heard that it was a home for girls, she had assumed it was an institution. What she found instead was a beautiful home that was beautifully furnished and kept clean. The thing that stunned her most was that she did not have to pay a thing to stay. She was even provided with clothes and personal items.

It was not only her physical surroundings that surprised her. Every person she met that first day took the time to hug her and talk to her. No one was turned off by the fact that she had just come out of a homeless shelter. Venus was overwhelmed. She had spent her entire life feeling unaccepted by the people closest to her and now strangers who had never met her before were welcoming her with open arms.

Venus was relieved that she finally had a safe place to stay where she did not have to worry about holding a job and paying bills while she endured a difficult pregnancy. Being at Mercy Ministries brought new hardships, however. She had to learn how to live in a house full of girls, many of whom were pregnant and going through the same hormonal changes she was going through. At 25 years old, she also had to face the issues that had brought her to this place in life. That was painful.

One afternoon, I was on my way home when I paused to play a little basketball with some of the girls who were outside. Venus approached me and asked if she could talk to me for a moment. She told me that Mercy Ministries was a wonderful program and she was glad that it existed, but she did not think that it was working for her.

I knew from experience that her feelings were common to many of the girls who come to us for help. It takes time for God to break through the walls they have built and help them understand that the way they want things done is not necessarily the way He is going to do them. The Bible says in Isaiah 55:9 that His ways and His thoughts are higher than ours. That means we have to trust Him to do what is right for us even when we do not understand the process He has chosen.

I asked Venus to set up a meeting with me so that we could discuss what she thought she needed. We talked the next day and she shared her opinion openly and honestly with me. I let her know that I was neither offended nor surprised by what she said and believed everything could be worked out in a way that would be beneficial to everyone.

At the end of our conversation, I asked Venus what it was that she really wanted to do in life. She did not even hesitate before responding that what she wanted most was to finish college. I was pleased to hear the determination in her voice. I told her that if she would work the program and graduate, I would make sure there was a way for her to go to school. That commitment was enough to make Venus agree to stay, but it did not make the process she had to go through any easier.

One of the first obstacles that stood in the way of her healing was the fact that she was convinced God could not or would not ever forgive her for having an abortion. Her counselor explained to her that there is no limit on God's forgiveness. In 1 John 1:9, we are promised that *If we confess our sins, he is faithful and just to forgive us our sins, and to cleanse us from all unrighteousness.* There are no barriers to receiving His forgiveness unless we choose not to ask Him for it.

Still hesitant, Venus studied King David's life. She read the story of his sin with Bathsheba, found in 2 Samuel 11-12. She saw that even though David committed adultery and murder and then tried to cover them both up, God forgave him when he humbled himself and confessed. He suffered consequences, but his choices did not cancel the plan that God had for his life.

Finally, after almost five years of living with extreme guilt and condemnation, Venus was able to ask God to forgive her. Almost immediately she began to experience His freedom. It seemed as if a weight was lifted from her. Her whole countenance changed and her attitude vastly improved. Venus believed, for the first time, that her life had worth. God still had a plan for her, in spite of her mistakes.

Even with that behind her, there was still much in her life that needed healing. She remained very angry about her situation in life. She was not angry at the child she carried, but she was angry that she was pregnant at all. Much of her anger was directed inward. She blamed herself heavily for all the poor choices that she had made.

In time, Venus began to see that while she was accountable for her decisions, she was also taking on false blame for choices that other people in her life had made. She learned to accept responsibility for the things she had done, ask God for His forgiveness, and then forgive herself. She also learned to forgive others for the role they had played in the hurtful situations.

One of the things that caused the most anger for her was the feeling that she had always been alone throughout her life. As a young girl, she had never found the protection and security that she sought from her family. That led to her decision to do everything on her own. When that failed, she felt betrayed. She tended to think that the world owed her because of the difficult circumstances she had been forced to survive.

God began to gently lead Venus to several passages of Scripture to show her that He had always been with her. Isaiah 43:2 (NIV) became very special to her. *When you pass through the waters, I will be with you; and when you pass through the rivers, they will not sweep over you. When you walk through the fire, you will not be burned; the flames will not set you ablaze.*

That verse helped Venus understand that while God had not promised to keep adversity from her life, He had promised to walk through it with her and keep her safe in spite of it all. He reminded her of the times that she had called on Him in her times of distress and He had rescued her, according to Psalm 81:7. She realized that she had not been forsaken. God had always been there, waiting for her to turn to Him. When she learned that, she was suddenly able to see evidence of His presence all around her. She began to trust Him.

In the meantime, her due date was fast approaching, and there was not a profile in our registry of prospective adoptive couples that matched her requirements. She wanted an African-American family to raise her child, since that was the heritage of both birthparents. There was not one black family in our files at that particular time. Venus gave birth to a healthy baby boy and named him Alexander. He was placed in foster care while we continued to trust God to provide the perfect family for him.

Her counselor and I began talking to families and churches, hoping that someone would know of a black family who wanted to adopt and would meet with Venus's approval. A few couples expressed interest, but when Venus interviewed them she was not satisfied. I knew that she had to be completely convinced that it was the right situation. We kept looking.

During this time, Venus struggled. The moment her son was born, she had fallen hopelessly in love with him. It was the first time that she had ever unconditionally loved anyone. Although she knew that God had told her to place Alexander for adoption, her overwhelming feelings for him made it difficult to do the right thing.

Old feelings of anger with God resurfaced. She did not understand why He would allow her to feel this way and then have her give the baby up. She also worried that Alexander would grow up thinking that his birthmother had rejected him. She did not want him to suffer from the thing that had been so damaging in her own life.

When a sinking depression began to envelop Venus, she found that so much of the Word had been put into her that it started coming out of her. She quoted every Scripture she could think of to remind herself that God was watching out for her and that He could be trusted. She knew that if His eye was on the sparrow, as the Bible says in Matthew 10:29, then He certainly saw what was happening in her life. If God took the time to number the hairs on her head (Matthew 10:30), then He had the time to listen to the cry of her heart.

She made up her mind that she was going to trust Him with all of her heart, and according to Proverbs 3:5-6, He would direct her paths. Much of her time was spent alone, digging into the Word and discovering more of His promises to protect and care for her. She refused to give in to any negative thoughts that presented themselves, choosing to take them captive and make them obedient to Christ (2 Corinthians 10:5). Then she replaced them with the Word of God and renewed her mind according to Romans 12:2. When she became discouraged, she went to a staff member who was able to talk and pray with her about the challenges she was facing.

Five months went by before the right family came along. There were several times when Venus almost decided to throw out the list of requirements she had made and just pick a family. I told her over and over again that she should not settle for less than what her heart desired. This was the most important decision she could make about her child and it had to be the one that God directed her to make. No matter how long it took, she had to wait for it to be right.

When the right family came along, there was no doubt in anyone's mind. From the minute Venus met with them, she knew that they were the parents God had chosen to raise her child. They were everything she had asked God for. Alexander was finally able to go home with his family. Venus was able to release him and her fears about how he would someday feel about her to the Lord. She knows that she did the right thing and believes that God will bless her for that.

Venus remained in the program for several months following Alexander's adoptive placement. With that area of her life settled, it was time to decide what was going to happen in the future. She knew she wanted to go back to school but also knew there were obstacles in the way. She began to pray, asking God for His direction and guidance for the next steps she should take.

While she was praying for God's direction, I was doing the same thing. I had committed to help her go to school and knew that we would do that. However, I needed to know how serious she was and whether or not she would be faithful. Jesus said in Luke 16:10 that he who is faithful in the little things will be made ruler over much. God led me to ask Venus to start working in the office for a few hours a week to see how she handled the little things.

Venus proved to be a hard worker and a fast learner. She was grateful for the chance to do something in return for all that she had been given, even though nothing was expected from her. Her integrity, gratefulness, and work ethic proved that she was trustworthy. I was convinced that Venus was a good investment.

Mercy Ministries paid off her old college loan out of our scholarship fund. That enabled her to apply for financial aid again. She applied to a school in the area and was accepted. The grant she received covered most of her tuition and a professor she met helped her get involved in a co-op program that provided the rest of what she needed. Her dream had finally come true!

Venus completed a year of school. Every week she sent a contribution to Mercy Ministries, even if it was only a few dollars. She had been taught about worshipping God through giving. She wanted to express her gratitude to God and to Mercy Ministries for the new life she had received.

During the summer she decided to work at a camp for abused and underprivileged children. I asked her to come with me one Sunday and give her testimony at Christ Church to the more than 5,000 who attend there weekly. She was happy to come, believing that it was an opportunity for her to give something back once again by sharing what God had done in her life.

What Venus did not know was that God was preparing to bless her for her faithfulness. Nelson Mazda of Nashville had donated a car to the ministry and they requested that it be given to a graduate who both needed it and could be trusted with it. Venus was the first girl who came to mind. She had spent her first year at school without a car, depending on others for rides, and had never complained.

I knew that she was transferring to a much bigger school that was farther away from town and needed her own car. She did not know how she would get one, but she simply believed that God would continue to provide for her. He did! At the podium that day, following her testimony, I handed her the keys to her very first car. It was a precious moment as several thousand people stood to their feet and applauded for a long time.

Venus is now in her third year of college, studying public relations. Her heart's desire is to use her degree and training to get the word out about places like Mercy Ministries to people who are in as desperate a situation as she once was. She believes that if she had known that an option like Mercy Ministries existed, she would not have chosen to go through with the abortion or to subject herself to the abuse that she did. There are many others who need to know that there is help available for the problems that face them, and Venus is willing to allow God to speak through her to reach them.

There are also many who need to know that God can be trusted. She loves to share the story of how she went from a girl who thought she would always have to care for herself to a young woman who brings all of her needs to God and allows Him to meet them. The challenge of letting go and surrendering her life to God was certainly difficult, but it has been worth it. He has given her more than she could ask, think, or imagine, according to Ephesians 3:20. Now, because of His incredible grace and mercy, it is her turn to touch others in His Name.

CHAPTER 6

VERONICA

Veronica stood on her front porch, locked out of her own house, frightened and confused. There was a crowd of people around her, telling her that her mother had a gun inside and that she was going to kill herself.

"Mom!" she screamed. "Mom, let me in! Please, let me in!"

Her mother had retreated to a room inside the house where no one could see her. The neighbors began to pull Veronica away from the door. "We'll go get some help," they said.

"I want to take the car," Veronica said. "If I don't take it, my mom will."

"You're not in any condition to drive," her neighbor told her. "Just come over to the house and we'll call someone."

Grudgingly Veronica went with them. Then, in the one moment when everyone's attention was focused away from her and the house, Veronica's mother ran out and jumped into the car.

"Mom! Don't leave me here!" Veronica screamed at the top of her lungs.

She did not even hesitate. Neighbors were standing in the way of the car, trying to stop her, but she drove over curbs and went barreling down the road.

Veronica ran after her a few steps and then collapsed in the street, sobbing. The pain inside her was overwhelming, so much more than from any of the abuse she had suffered or any of the times she had tried to hurt herself. Her mother, the one person in the world whom she desperately loved, had just driven off and abandoned her completely. Veronica had never felt so alone in her life.

The neighbors picked her up from the street and took her back to their house. Three hours later her mom called.

"Sorry honey," she said, her voice light. "I just had to get away. Hope you didn't mind."

Veronica was frightened by the fact that, although it was probably the most traumatic thing she had ever been through, to her mother, it was not even a big deal.

"I'll understand if you don't want to come home," her mother said. "You can stay away for a while if you want to."

It was like she had been dealt another blow. Now her mother did not even want her at home with her anymore. Veronica knew she could not go back to her mother's. She would run away, like she always had and probably always would.

Veronica was born in a small, rural town of about 1,200 people. Growing up in a town that size meant that everyone knew everyone else and almost everyone was concerned about putting on a good show for the nosy neighbors. Veronica's family did well in the unspoken competition to see who lived in the biggest house, drove the nicest cars, and whose children behaved the best in public.

Veronica, her parents, and her older sister attended church regularly. Her father often sang at church and tended to be the center of attention. He was well respected in the community. At home, however, he was a different man. He constantly intimidated his wife and children and was an expert at manipulating and controlling them.

It was like she had two different fathers. At church, people would approach her and tell her how wonderful her father was and how lucky she was to have him. She had to smile bravely, all the while screaming on the inside for someone to understand. They lived this double life for sixteen years, putting on a face in public that was very different from the one worn inside the home.

Her father used to tell her that it was a privilege to be in their family, and if she did not do what it took to be a part of the family, she could go somewhere else. She determined in her heart that she would do whatever it took to stay there. She never told anyone how he would fly into rages at home over the smallest things and how it was always his wife's fault or the kids' fault. The abuse that she witnessed or suffered stayed locked up inside of her.

He would constantly grab Veronica and shake her. Her arms would ache all day long after one brief encounter with her father and his huge hands. Sometimes she was slapped or thrown to the floor. Once she was thrown all the way across the kitchen, landing in a stairwell and rolling down the rest of the stairs. To this day, Veronica has trouble with her jaw and has had surgery on both sides to correct the problems caused by her father grabbing her by the chin in his crushing grip.

There was sexual abuse, too, although Veronica is still unable to talk about the details. She remembers coming home from school and hiding from her father in the basement. He always found her. He would come downstairs at night, telling his wife he was getting his vitamins, and instead go into Veronica's room to "say goodnight."

Starting in the sixth grade, Veronica thought of ways to kill herself, creating suicide plans but never following through. At age twelve she began running into things and cutting herself, purposely causing physical pain. There was so much happening inside her emotionally that injuring her body seemed to be the only way she could release some of the turmoil.

She had to give herself a reason to feel the pain and needed something else on which to concentrate. Veronica also believed she had to punish herself for the mistakes she made. Her father was a perfectionist and she had picked up much of that from him. When she did something wrong, rather than waiting for someone else to punish her, she chose to hurt herself.

When Veronica was thirteen, her sister came home and told her that she was getting married and would be moving out of the house. Even though they had never been particularly close due to a four year age difference, Veronica burst into tears. She wanted to be happy for her sister, but she was terrified of being the one left behind in the house. Five days after she graduated, Veronica's sister was married and gone.

Veronica was miserable without her. She began looking for ways to get out as well. Just after that school year ended, Veronica was looking through the newspaper and saw an ad for a job at a horse stable, two hours away. She showed it to her mother and they packed her bags and drove down there.

From the first, it was evident that there was something wrong with the situation. Veronica was only fourteen years old and did not have a worker's permit, but no one questioned that. Her mother was not allowed to see the sleeping quarters where her daughter would be staying and Veronica soon found out why. Eight girls stayed in the back room of an old run-down farmhouse that was in horrible condition. Still, Veronica wanted to escape her home so badly that she was willing to stay, and her mother was so emotionally unstable that she allowed Veronica to be there rather than at home.

The owner physically abused the girls, and the boys who worked there often sexually harassed them. That summer, most of the girls quit but Veronica stuck it out, determined to stay away from home. One weekend she was in the farmhouse by herself and two of the boys, who were eighteen and twenty years old, attempted to force themselves on her. Veronica was able to get away and lock herself behind a door, but another scar was left.

After the summer ended and Veronica returned home, she slipped into major depression. One afternoon, when she was in the ninth grade, she ran away and started hiking through a park near the school. She had a knife in her hand and had already begun cutting on her arms. She was planning to kill herself, or at least run very far away. A group of boys on the mountainside setting up forestry signs saw her. Once they realized what she was doing, they chased her, caught her, and called for the school counselor.

The counselor recommended inpatient treatment, and although Veronica's parents were infuriated and insisted that it was simply attention-seeking behavior, she chose to go into treatment rather than to remain at home. She stayed there for about thirty days and was released without much improvement. That started a cycle in Veronica's life of going from anti-depressant to anti-depressant, from counselor to counselor. There were several more serious suicide attempts where she overdosed on drugs. She constantly experimented with mixing prescription drugs and alcohol, wondering if she could find the right combination that would end her life

In the meantime, her parents' relationship was crumbling. Veronica's mother chose to make her daughter her confidant. She told Veronica all kinds of things that she did not want to hear, both about her father and her own relationships with various boyfriends. Divorce proceedings began when Veronica was sixteen and the whole town became involved and took sides.

People were shocked to discover that this family with such a perfect image was actually in turmoil. Veronica's father was very good at gaining sympathy for himself and people began turning against her mother. She began to drink heavily, even taking Veronica to the liquor store with her one afternoon and telling her to pick out a pack of wine coolers for herself. Veronica gladly accepted, welcoming the opportunity to escape the chaos around her at least for a little while.

Eventually, Veronica's mother started to see an old boyfriend who was already married. When Veronica's father found out about the relationship, he confronted the boyfriend and threatened to tell the pastor of the church where they were all members. Veronica's mother was infuriated and called her estranged husband. During the course of the angry phone call, she made the comment that if he were to expose her new relationship, he should be prepared to sing at her funeral.

Seeing a chance to further damage his wife's reputation, Veronica's father called the neighbors and told them that she had a gun and was threatening to kill herself. That was when Veronica's mother locked herself inside the house and eventually drove away, leaving Veronica behind. Veronica moved in with another family for a few months, then came home for several weeks. From then on, she was constantly moving in and out of her house.

Veronica's mother was free for the first time, making her own decisions which were leading her down a wild and destructive path. She was drinking more and more heavily and becoming involved in the bar scene. Still dating a married man, she wanted time alone with him. Veronica knew if she came home and saw his truck in the driveway that she was not allowed to come into the house. She would grow frustrated with her mother's behavior and move out, staying with different friends off and on, but she always felt guilty for abandoning her mother and returned home.

One night Veronica was experiencing such stress that she suffered an excruciatingly painful migraine headache. She blacked out and when she woke up she could not see. Her mother was gone and Veronica was alone in the house with no one to help her. Finally she was able to contact her sister who came and took her to the hospital.

The doctors wanted to do a spinal tap because Veronica's temperature had spiked and they could not determine what was wrong. In order to do that they needed parental permission for the strong drugs Veronica would be given. Unable to find their mother, Veronica's sister had to call their father. He gave permission for the drugs and then showed up at the emergency room. While Veronica was heavily sedated he took advantage of the opportunity to sexually abuse her once again.

Around this time, Veronica developed an eating disorder. In the past, she had decided to quit eating for a week at a time, in an attempt to get her father's attention and show him she was angry with him. He never noticed and she gave up. As a junior in high school, she would stop eating for periods of up to two weeks. Her mother would sometimes question whether she was anorexic but never pushed the issue. Desperate for her mother's love and attention, Veronica continued with her behavior.

There did not seem to be any hope for Veronica. She could not find anyone who cared enough about her to simply listen. In total despair one evening, when no one else was home, Veronica went out into the garage. She found a glass bottle and smashed it, driving the jagged edges into both wrists. The cuts were so deep in one arm that she could actually see veins and arteries.

As the blood dripped down her arms, Veronica became extremely frightened. She went inside the house and found rags, tore them up, and used them as bandages. Although she lost a good deal of blood and was in great pain, she never sought medical attention for the gashes. No one in her family ever noticed them, in spite of the fact that she could not bend her wrists for several weeks. Today she still bears the physical scars from that attempt on her life.

Less than four months after the divorce was final, Veronica's mother remarried. It was the summer before Veronica's senior year. She had no privacy in her home with her stepfather there. There was no door to her bedroom and her space was constantly invaded. Once again, she felt like the least important person in her family and the one who was constantly overlooked in favor of everyone else's needs. She continued to move in and out of her house, always looking for a real escape.

Over the Christmas break, Veronica went on an overnight shopping trip into a nearby city with a friend. They met up with her friend's boyfriend and his roommate. The two men were house sitting in the city and the four went back to that house. Veronica and her friend began partying with alcohol and marijuana, and eventually Veronica's friend disappeared into a bedroom with her boyfriend and passed out.

Veronica was left alone with the other man. She was afraid and uncomfortable but did not want to leave. Her friend was still there and Veronica was afraid she would be angry with her if she left. Against her better judgment, she stayed. The man violently raped Veronica that night.

Two days later, still in unbelievable pain, Veronica finally went to the hospital. The police told her that it would be kept confidential so she filed a report. No charges were brought against the man because Veronica's friend was in the house the whole time. The authorities told her that the case would never stand up in court. Veronica let it go, just wanting the whole thing to be over.

Unfortunately, an officer called her home looking for her before she got there and ended up telling her mother the whole story. By the time Veronica got home, her mother had called her father and he was at the house waiting for her. He told her it was her own fault. He told her she had been in the house with the guy, therefore she had asked for it and should not have the nerve to accuse him of rape. Her mother was no more sympathetic, asking Veronica who she thought would help her if she were pregnant. They punished her because she had been raped, taking her car away and not allowing her to use the phone. Devastated by the lack of family support once again, Veronica moved out.

Finally she graduated from high school and for the summer went away to a Christian camp for girls she had heard about at a concert. Someone was able to sponsor her trip, including the cost of transportation. While there, Veronica opened up to a counselor about issues in her life that she had never discussed before. One of the counselors there attended Christ Church in Nashville and when she heard Veronica's story, she knew she needed to come to Mercy Ministries. She requested an application for her and Veronica was accepted into the program.

When she first came to Mercy Ministries, Veronica was a broken young woman. She was not prepared to give up some of the things she had held on to for so long. She was not used to having structure in her life, to being told what she could and could not do and when she could do it. For years she had just picked up and moved whenever she wanted to, or whenever things were too difficult for her to handle.

Suddenly she was being confronted with her issues and forced to deal with them if she wanted to get better. She was also unable to get by with the manipulative and controlling behavior she had learned to use to get the attention she craved. Although she knew that the people confronting her were doing it because they cared about her, she felt she could not handle the pressure. Frustrated, she ran away.

Veronica moved to another state where she got a job and began attending college. Her depression grew worse as did her eating disorder. She would go for a month at a time without eating and then she would slip into bingeing and purging. She abused laxatives and forced herself to throw up, often using Ipecac to rid herself of the food she had eaten. Blood vessels in her face would burst from the force of throwing up so violently. Even though she knew the damage she was doing to her body, she could not stop.

Eventually the depression and the eating disorder were both affecting her so deeply that she could not get out of bed in the morning. She went into another treatment center and then on to a different school. Her roommates were terrified by her continued eating disorder behavior and consistently asked the resident advisor and director to take Veronica to the hospital. Veronica was to the point where she hoped each hospital trip would be her last, wishing she could just die so it would be over. Finally, she collapsed in her dorm and had to be rushed to the hospital by ambulance. The school asked her to leave.

Giving up on her dream of going to college, Veronica returned to Nashville with a friend and tried to work. She could not hold a job. She wanted to die more every day. The only thing that kept her from ending her life was a sobering fear that if she committed suicide she would go to hell.

Eventually, her misery became so intense that even the fear of hell was not enough to dissuade her. She took a severe overdose while sitting in a park one afternoon. After she swallowed the pills, she went through her Bible and read every verse on forgiveness that she could find, hoping that would be enough to get her into heaven. As she sat there, waiting to die, everything began to get blurry and her heart started to race. The fear that she would go to hell seized her once again and she dragged herself to her car. Somehow she found her way to an emergency room.

Four days later Veronica woke up in the intensive care unit, attached to intravenous tubes and a heart monitor, with an oxygen tube in her nose. She finally realized that God would not let her die. She knew she had taken enough medicine to "kill a cow" and had survived without any permanent damage. For some reason God had spared her life once more and she decided she should find out His plan if she could.

I saw Veronica after a church service, just a few days after her release from the hospital. She asked if she could come back to Mercy Ministries. I told her that I thought it was possible, but that if she did come back she would have to quickly prove that she was serious. There would be no more game playing or manipulative behavior. If she truly wanted help, she would have to be completely honest with the staff and work hard at facing her issues, no matter how painful.

Veronica had already made the decision that there was nothing else for her to do but to get better. She finally felt that she wanted to live but everything in her life was still in shambles. There was no communication between her and her family and she had no one to whom she could turn for help. I later found out that Veronica had spent a few days sleeping in her car at a truck stop while she waited to find out if she would be accepted into the program.

Once Veronica came back into the program for the second time, things began to happen quickly for her. Much of the foundation for her healing had already been laid during the few months she had spent with us her first time in the program. The first area in which she achieved victory was with her eating disorder.

Veronica's brushes with death had taught her the truth of Jeremiah 29:11 (NIV), in which the Lord declares, *I know the plans I have for you, plans to prosper you and not to harm you, plans to give you hope and a future*. She was certain that God had not let her die because there was something He intended for her to do. If that was true, then she was going to have to take care of herself so that she would be ready to fulfill God's call on her life.

She suddenly understood that the eating disorder was wrecking her body. As she became immersed in the Word, she began to change the thought patterns that had held her in bondage for so many years. Her counselors helped her to identify her ungodly beliefs and replace them with the truth. Rather than being critical and harsh towards herself, Veronica began to believe that she was fearfully and wonderfully made, just as the Word says in Psalm 139. She accepted that she was made in God's image and that He loved her for who she was.

Veronica's behavior was changing, but there was still something more that she needed. The revelation came to her clearly, so suddenly one day that she knew it had to be from God. Suddenly, she knew that part of His purpose for her life, His reason for keeping her alive, was so that she could touch others who had suffered what she had. In 2 Corinthians 1:4 we are reminded that one of the reasons God comforts us is so we can comfort others. Once she was finally able to understand that there were people out there whom she could help if she could see beyond herself and her own problems, Veronica had the motivation she needed to conquer the eating disorder.

With that part of her life coming under control, God began to touch other areas of Veronica's heart that she thought were dead and gone. For so long Veronica's feelings had been completely numb. She desperately wanted to know what it was like to feel hope again. She was learning to believe that God's Word was true in spite of her feelings but still longed for some type of emotion other than pain.

One night, during a youth service at church, Veronica went forward during the altar call to pray and ask God to restore her feelings. After about five minutes of feeling nothing, she became frustrated and sat down. "God," she thought, "that's it. I tried. You're going to have to come to me."

Less than five minutes passed before a young man, one of the youth leaders in the congregation, came up to her as she sat in the pew and asked if he could pray for her. Shocked, Veronica agreed. He prayed with her, speaking to her directly about the issues she was facing and a number of other things that he could not possibly have known if God had not been speaking to him. Veronica sobbed as the young man told her that God had a purpose for her. It was a major turning point in her healing. It was the first time she believed that God really did care for her and that she could face the future.

Other major breakthroughs came quickly for Veronica after that. She was able to deal with her issues of codependency and insecurity. Since her parents had never really been there for her while growing up, Veronica had begun to cling to anyone who appeared to pay her attention. She felt like she had used up all the grace of her friends who had at one time been willing to help her. Now she had to learn to trust in God more than people and to let Him be her security in life.

Veronica was also able to truly forgive her father. She wrote him a letter, amazing herself that, for the first time, she could offer him forgiveness without expecting him to take responsibility for the things he had done to her. She had written to him before, but they had been angry and bitter letters full of accusations and demands that he apologize to her and her mother and sister for his behavior.

This time there were no strings attached. She told him that she forgave him and was able to leave his response in God's hands. She had learned the truth about forgiveness. It does not excuse wrong behavior; it simply frees us to go on with our lives without being tied down to past hurts. Jesus reminds us in Mark 11:25 that we must forgive one another in order to receive forgiveness from God. When we hold on to things that have hurt us, we only damage ourselves and our own relationships with God. We must release those painful things into God's hands and trust Him to deal with them in His own way.

All these decisions were keys to Veronica's healing and she dedicated herself to doing all that God called her to do. She had lived up to the condition that she had to prove that she was serious about the program and she even became a leader among the girls. Her diligence was rewarded. Within four months, Veronica was prepared to graduate from Mercy Ministries.

For the last several years, ever since contemporary Christian artists Point of Grace have supported the cause of Mercy Ministries, I have toured nationwide with them and shared the vision of Mercy Ministries during each concert. It has been an incredible opportunity as many girls have learned about the program through the concerts and made the decision to come and receive help. In addition, many people have joined our family of supporters through hearing about Mercy Ministries at a concert. Because of the growth of the ministry and the addition of new homes, it has become necessary to send someone else to travel with Point of Grace and share about Mercy Ministries. At the time of Veronica's graduation, I was praying about selecting a graduate to tour with Point of Grace and give her testimony from the stage each night as part of the concert.

God prompted me to ask Veronica to consider making this commitment. She was terrified, wondering if she might be putting herself in a position where she would be subject to ridicule by sharing intimate details of her life with complete strangers and making herself vulnerable on a daily basis. In spite of her fears, however, she accepted the challenge, trusting that it was yet another piece of God's plan for her life.

Although she initially had her doubts, she began to see how her testimony was helping others. After a concert in Florida, she was able to lead a young girl to Christ. Several young women she met at concerts have come into the program. At each concert, as she stood up to tell her story, she reminded herself that people who were going through some of the turmoil that she endured were going to hear her speak. Perhaps they would realize that if God had brought Veronica through, He would do the same for them.

Veronica is now going back to college to complete her degree. She wants to learn more about how to depend on God, not on herself or others. The most important thing to her is not to be in the spotlight, but to know God and to know that in her daily walk with Him, she is pleasing Him and impacting others for His glory.

She knows now that her life is just beginning. Every day, God seems to reveal a little bit more of the path that He has laid out for her life. She continues to abide by Proverbs 3:5-6, trusting in the Lord with all of her heart and leaning not upon her own understanding, but in all her ways acknowledging Him. He is directing her path.

With an unshakable understanding of how God can take everything that is meant for evil and turn it into good (Genesis 45:5), Veronica is able to continually reach out to others. She allows the healing that God brought into her life to overflow. Her life is a true example of the "ripple effect." As one life is changed and she uses what she has learned to impact others, the power of God's healing touch is endlessly multiplied.

CHAPTER 7

KEVIN & LISA

*S*he closed her bedroom door behind her carefully and quickly settled down in the middle of her bed. A rush of emotions filled her heart: excitement, fear, hope, pain. Carefully she opened the large envelope and slid out the binder that held the most important information she would ever consider.

The letter on the first page of the notebook began "Dear Birthmother," and her eyes filled up with tears. She knew adoption was the right decision for her and her boyfriend to make, but knowing that it was right did not make it any easier to do.

Her mother had passed away almost three years prior, and as she sought to ease the pain, in hopes of filling the void, she made some wrong choices and found herself facing an unplanned pregnancy. When she first found out, she was both excited and scared. She and her boyfriend thought that they could keep the baby. They truly loved each other and he was going to quit college and start working to provide for them.

Then she started having complications with the pregnancy. The second ultrasound discovered that she was actually pregnant with twins. That really scared her. She had wondered if they could take care of one baby, but she knew they could not provide for two babies. They agreed that adoption was the best option for them and their children.

She continued reading the letter, and as she learned more about the couple who wanted to adopt her twins, an unspeakable sense of peace settled over her. Reading the stories they told about their families as they grew up was like reading about her own childhood. They had lots of brothers and sisters.

There was even a story about riding in the family station wagon for summer vacation that was just like she remembered.

It was too good to be true. This family was perfect—they had everything she wanted her babies to have, right down to another set of twins in the family. They were God-sent. It was obvious that God's hand had been on this situation from the beginning.

She finished the letter and turned the page to look at the pictures. The smiling faces of a beautiful couple looked back at her. She blinked and looked again, and her heart leapt. She knew them! Although she had never actually met them, she knew who they were, and there was no one better she could think of to raise her precious babies.

There are many times in our lives when God is at work, even while we are unaware of His hand in action. Events that occur or people we meet in passing can be quickly forgotten until a circumstance down the road brings it back to our memory. Then we realize that something more than a mere coincidence has happened. We understand that what we thought was chance was actually a part of God's intricate plan for our lives.

My role as founder and president of Mercy Ministries of America allows me many opportunities for such "coincidences" to occur. There are many people I have met in my years of speaking about the ministry who, even though it may have been a brief introduction or a fleeting conversation at first, have become intimately connected with the ministry in an unforgettable way which could only be the handiwork of God.

The family of the late Pastor John Osteen from Lakewood Church in Houston, Texas, is one such example. I had highly respected Pastor Osteen for many years, using his teachings by video in the classroom with the girls in the program, almost from the beginning of the ministry. His wife's incredible testimony of being healed from cancer has encouraged many people. For a long time I admired him and his family from a distance.

In 1993 I was invited to speak at a missions conference where Pastor Osteen's wife, Dodie, and their daughter, Lisa, were also ministering. I was amazed by Dodie and Lisa. They had the ability to make each one of the people attending the conference feel that he or she was a special part of the service.

Dodie and Lisa were very excited to learn about Mercy Ministries and the opportunities provided to hurting young women. I had the chance to personally meet them and sign copies of my first book, *Echoes of Mercy*, for them. Later, after returning home from the conference, I received a personal note from Dodie, thanking me and stating how thrilled she was to hear about the work God was doing. I was amazed that she would take time out of her busy schedule to personally write me.

The relationship between the two ministries continued to grow. In 1995, I spoke at a Point of Grace concert that was held at Lakewood Church. The day of the concert, Pastor Osteen's personal assistant approached me and asked if I would pray with the Osteens' daughter, Lisa, and her husband, Kevin. They were believing God for a baby but they had not yet been able to conceive. I was thrilled at the opportunity to pray for them and a seed was planted in my heart.

More than two years later, at a Joyce Meyer conference, a pastor's wife asked me if I would spend some time with a girl in their church. She was a young woman whose mother had died of cancer a year earlier, and who had been struggling since then. She and her boyfriend had made some mistakes, and they had recently discovered that she was pregnant.

I met with this young woman and her boyfriend for about two hours. I told them that God was proud of them for choosing to have the baby rather than choosing an abortion. I also told them that Mercy Ministries could help them through the process of deciding whether they wanted to place the baby for adoption or parent the child themselves.

They needed time to think things over. They were scared and did not know what they were going to do, but both of them truly wanted to do the right thing. I provided them with the same materials that girls in the program use as they try to make their decision to parent or place their children and left them to think it through and pray about it.

About a month after that initial meeting, the young woman called to touch base with me. She said that she and the birthfather were leaning toward adoption, although they had not made a firm decision yet. Her desire was to go to Bible school and she was not sure that she could parent and do that as well. Both her family and the birthfather's family were in agreement with the decision to begin pursuing an adoptive placement.

Years ago, God had clearly instructed me on how the process of adoption was to be handled at Mercy Ministries. Every girl who came to the ministry because of an unplanned pregnancy was to be honored for making the choice to allow her child to live. First and foremost, each girl was to be allowed to make her own decision. The staff was responsible for providing each girl with the information needed to make a good decision, but it was ultimately between the girl and God whether she parented or placed her child for adoption.

Second, God showed me that the way He would lead me to the right couple for each child was to ask the birthparents to make a list of what was in their hearts regarding adoptive parents for their child. They could list the age range, nationality, geographic area, family size, occupation, and any other qualities they desired in adoptive parents. The staff would then take that list, compare it to the profiles of couples who had applied to adopt, and find several matches for the girl and the birthfather, if he was involved, to consider.

This is the procedure that is followed each time an adoption is handled through Mercy Ministries of America. Although this particular young woman was not coming into the program, the same policy was followed in her situation. I encouraged her to continue praying about it and told her that God would let her know for sure His will for her and her child. I also asked her to start thinking about what kind of characteristics she wanted the adoptive couple to have and to make a detailed list.

Another month passed before I received a second phone call from the young woman. She had just been to the doctor and found out that she was actually pregnant with twins! In her heart, the fact that she was pregnant with twins was confirmation that adoption was the right decision. She and the birthfather were sure that they wanted to proceed with a placement through Mercy Ministries.

A few days later, the birthparents sent me their list of desired characteristics in a couple. It was the most specific list I had ever seen! They wanted a couple who was under forty years old and unable to have their own children so that these would be their first. Both parents were to be involved somehow in full-time ministry and from an interdenominational Word and Spirit church in the South.

The adoptive couple had to be financially able to provide well for the children. The birthparents also wanted their children to have a large, close extended family, with lots of aunts and uncles and cousins and grandparents. Not only did they want lots of family members around, but their final request was that there be a set of twins somewhere in that family.

I took the list and had it compared to the files of adoptive couples who had applied to Mercy Ministries. It was so specific that there was not one family in the registry who matched all of the qualities the birthparents requested. Knowing that God would provide the right family in His time, I made the adoptive placement a matter of prayer.

Several days after receiving the list, I was preparing for a youth rally at which I was scheduled to speak. As I tried to focus on the upcoming event, my thoughts were continually drawn to the young woman and her situation. Knowing that no couple had yet applied who matched the characteristics, I tried to put it out of my mind and concentrate on what God wanted me to say to the youth in just a few hours.

However, it seemed that God would not let it go. Time after time, the situation came back into my thoughts. Finally, in frustration, I cried out, "God, whose babies are these?" Immediately, God dropped two names into my heart: Kevin and Lisa.

Just as quickly, my mind began the reasoning process. I had not seen or been in touch personally with them since Pastor Osteen's assistant had asked me to pray with them three years earlier. They had never applied to the ministry to adopt, and I did not even know whether or not they had been able to have their own children. As far as I knew, there were no twins in the family, so they would not meet the criteria even if they did want to adopt.

I set the matter aside temporarily in order to preach at the youth service. While there, I saw the daughter of Dr. Mark Barclay, Dawn, and her husband, Jim. Dr. Barclay is the pastor of a large church in Midland, Michigan, where I have spoken several times. I knew that the Barclays were good friends with the Osteens so I asked Dawn if she knew if Kevin and Lisa had any children. To my surprise, Dawn said that she had just been to Lakewood Church in Houston with her parents three weeks prior to our conversation. While they were at Lakewood, Kevin and Lisa asked Dr. Barclay to pray for them because they had been unable to have children. After Dr. Barclay prayed over them, he said to Kevin and Lisa, *I see you with children soon, and don't be surprised if God gives you twins!*

I knew that this information was confirmation from God. I told Dawn and Jim why I was asking, but requested they say nothing to Kevin and Lisa. Although I was sure now of God's leading, I was hesitant to contact them about it. Logically it seemed to be the backwards way of doing things.

I sought advice from my pastor in Louisiana, Pastor Sam Carr. Brother Sam is the vice-president of the Board of Trustees of Mercy Ministries and regularly advises me on spiritual and practical matters. He and his wife, Becky, adopted a baby from Mercy Ministries several years ago, and Becky served as our adoptions coordinator for a time. Brother Sam agreed that it seemed to be the Lord's leading to pursue Kevin and Lisa and encouraged me to go ahead.

I finally called Lisa at Lakewood Church. I spent about fifteen minutes, non-stop, telling Lisa the whole story of meeting the birthmother, her situation, and the list of requirements the young couple had submitted. Finally, I told Lisa that it seemed that she and Kevin met every qualification on the list, except for the fact that there were no twins in the family, but not to let that stop them if they were interested. I was about to ask the birthmother to consider dropping the "twin in the family" requirement anyway.

"Nancy," Lisa said, "you've forgotten. Kevin has a twin sister!"

Momentarily, I was stunned. "Do you think you and Kevin might be interested?" I asked.

"Absolutely!" Lisa replied.

She immediately went to Kevin's office and told him the story. They had been trying unsuccessfully to conceive for six years. Kevin had been asking Lisa for the past year to call me regarding adoption. The week before I called, Lisa had asked God to move supernaturally in their lives and show them if that was the route He wanted them to go. My call was the confirmation she had sought.

Kevin had always desired and prayed that he and his wife would have twins. He asked Lisa to call me back right away to find out the process they would need to go through in order to proceed with the adoption. He and Lisa prayed about it further and began to complete the necessary forms and the required home study.

After about a week, they let Lisa's parents know what their plans were. They were thrilled! Kevin and Lisa told no one else except a few close friends and the attorney and social worker who helped them with the paperwork. The adoption and home study required a number of documents, including medical reports and biographical sketches on each of them. Kevin and Lisa set about getting everything ready for their new family.

Meanwhile, I communicated with the birthmother to let her know that there was a couple who met all their desired characteristics. They were thrilled and eager to review the profile. As soon as Kevin and Lisa got all of their information together, I forwarded it to the young woman and the babies' father.

All of the information in prospective adoptive parent profiles is non-identifying, meaning that last names are not given and details about the location of the family are very vague. Still, when the birthmother received Kevin and Lisa's profile, she called me to say that she knew who they were because she recognized them in the pictures. Knowing who they were made the young woman even more sure that this was God's plan. She thought it was too good to be true. Her family knew of and respected the entire Osteen family and their ministry.

Although I was excited for the young woman and her certainty that this was what God was leading her to do, I was also concerned for Kevin and Lisa. Traditional adoptions are often rooted in fear of the "what ifs" that can be involved. Adoptive couples may fear that birthparents might change their minds, or that someone from the agency could inadvertently release personal information about them and they could be located.

In a Mercy Ministries adoption, the girls and the adoptive couples come to an agreement about how much contact they want to have and how much information is to be shared. It was unusual that the birthparents would know so much about the adoptive family, but we had all known that the possibility existed due to the national television outreach and international missions impact of the ministry of Lakewood Church.

I immediately called Kevin and Lisa to let them know that the birthparents knew who they were. Understandably, this information concerned them. I took that opportunity to minister to them about fear. First John 4:18 says that perfect love drives out all fear. The birthmother was doing her best to love perfectly by choosing unselfishly to give up her babies, knowing it was best for them. She was trusting God that Kevin and Lisa would love these children as their own. It was so clear that God had orchestrated every detail of this process so far. Kevin and Lisa decided that they were willing to proceed. They too trusted in God's perfect love for them, therefore dispelling all fear.

Once the initial paperwork was in place, it became a waiting game. Everyone involved was praying that the birthmother would make it to

35 weeks before going into labor so that the babies would be well developed. She had already gone into premature labor three times. The doctor had to put sutures in her cervix and put her on bed rest for the duration of the pregnancy.

While they waited, Kevin and Lisa focused on praying for the birthmother and the babies, and on getting everything ready for their babies to come home. Lisa and her sister went shopping for everything they could think of that they might need, and Lisa took full advantage of "twin discounts" that some stores offer.

Finally, at 4:45 on a Saturday morning, I awakened Kevin and Lisa with a phone call to say that the birthmother was in labor and on her way to the hospital. God had answered their prayers—she had made it to 36 weeks and it was time! Knowing that it would be at least several more hours before they heard anything more, Kevin and Lisa tried to go on with their day in spite of their overwhelming excitement.

At 9:52 a.m., Kevin was getting ready to leave the health club when he paused and looked at the clock. Noting the time, he thought, "I need to start watching the clock to remember what I was doing when the babies were born." Around the same time, as Lisa was reading her Bible, she stopped and prayed for the birthmother's delivery and the babies.

At 10:15 a.m., I called to tell them that the twins had been born three minutes apart, at 9:52 and 9:55 a.m.! They were both girls. The first baby, who Kevin and Lisa named Catherine Ann, weighed 5 pounds and 11 ounces. The second, named Caroline Grace, weighed 4 pounds and 13 ounces. Both girls were healthy and the birthmother had done extremely well during the delivery. Kevin and Lisa called their family to let them know the good news and then spent the day doing some final shopping and packing.

The next day, after church, Kevin and Lisa traveled to the city where the girls had been born and met me there. The babies had been scheduled to be released from the hospital the following day, but that morning we discovered that neither baby was maintaining normal body temperature. They could not yet leave the hospital. I took Kevin and Lisa to the hospital to meet their babies for the first time.

They were both amazed by how beautiful the girls were. The nurses kept them in the same warmer because they liked being together. Once, when Caroline would not stop crying, the nurse put her in with Catherine. They locked arms and slept peacefully and have been kept together ever since! Kevin and Lisa were able to hold the girls, and Lisa was allowed to feed and burp Caroline. They stayed for about thirty minutes in the nursery and had a hard time leaving.

The birthparents learned that Kevin and Lisa were at the hospital and asked to meet them. It had previously been agreed that they would meet when the birthparents handed the babies to the adoptive parents, but Kevin and Lisa changed their plan and talked with them. I joined them as they met for the first time.

Everyone hugged as they came in and they spent a few minutes talking. Lisa noticed how young they both looked and that they were a bit shy. She and Kevin assured the birthparents that they would take good care of the girls and expressed their appreciation for the unselfish and loving decision the young couple had made. The birthmother's father stopped by to talk with Kevin and Lisa as well. All of the young woman's family was familiar with Pastor Osteen's ministry, and everyone seemed confident that this was the family God had chosen to raise the babies.

What we did not know at the time was that the birthmother and her boyfriend had almost decided not to go through with the adoptive placement. After spending some time with the babies, they thought maybe it would be best to keep them and raise them. That was one reason why they asked to meet with Kevin and Lisa before the arranged time.

Following that meeting, though, both the young woman and her boyfriend had a true peace about their decision. They knew the babies would be well taken care of and loved, and they were able to turn their daughters over into the care of the people God had chosen to be the parents.

It was two more days before the girls were able to leave the hospital. The afternoon they were released, Kevin and Lisa met with the birthparents, the birthmother's father, and the pastors at the church where I had first spoken with the young woman seven months earlier. Both Kevin and Lisa expressed their gratitude again, and Kevin prayed a beautiful prayer over the birthparents, reminding them that God always rewards people who give willingly. This was the best gift that could ever be given and God would give back to them many times over, just as He promises in Luke 6:38.

The birthparents cried as they handed the babies to Kevin and Lisa, along with special gifts for each of the girls. They were beautifully dressed in light pink cotton dresses with white collars, islet bonnets, and crocheted shoes. Kevin and Lisa committed to pray for the birthparents regularly. Immediately, they changed the babies' diapers and fed them in the pastor's office. The girls were finally theirs!

It was another six days before Kevin and Lisa were able to leave the hotel due to the paperwork and legalities that needed to be completed. They spent their time feeding the babies, changing diapers, washing bottles and clothes, and enjoying every minute of it! Family members drove over to meet the babies and visit with Kevin and Lisa.

Finally, when the girls were ten days old, all the papers were signed and Kevin and Lisa had approval to take the babies home. When they arrived at their house, their entire family was there with birthday cakes for the girls to welcome them! Different family members visited throughout the week, fulfilling the birthparents' requests for an active and loving extended family.

Until this point, only a few people outside the family knew anything about the adoption. Most people had been told that Kevin and Lisa were away handling some business arrangements. They wanted to be sure that everything was in place before they made it public knowledge. Two weeks after the girls were brought home, on Father's Day, they were finally introduced to the congregation of Lakewood Church.

Dodie Osteen, the proud grandmother, stood before the congregation and explained the church's involvement with Mercy Ministries and how God had connected the two some years back. She told the story of my meeting with the birthmother and her list of requirements, leaving out the final one regarding twins in the family. At that point, she introduced Catherine Ann, and Lisa's youngest sister, April, brought her out to her parents and to meet her new church family. The whole church erupted in ecstatic cheers, knowing how long Kevin and Lisa had believed God for the child they now held in their arms.

Then Dodie explained the final requirement, and what a blessing it was that Kevin had a twin sister, since three minutes after Catherine Ann had arrived, Caroline Grace was born! The same proud Aunt April brought her out to join the rest of her family. The congregation of 8,000 exploded in applause and cheers once again, rejoicing over their double portion! Pastor Osteen prayed over his newest grand-daughters to dedicate them to the Lord. The work that God had begun many years ago was finally complete.

Kevin and Lisa have enjoyed every moment of parenthood. Both of them got up together during the night when the babies were first home, and each would feed a twin. Kevin is one of the most active fathers that Lisa has ever seen, kissing the girls a thousand times a day and even making diaper-changing an event! He is a true hands-on dad, instrumental in raising them and praying over them.

Pastor John Osteen had prayed for so many years for Kevin and Lisa to have children and was a constant source of encouragement to Lisa, always telling her that she would one day be a mother. These precious babies were a fulfillment of all those years of prayer. In January of 1999, not long after the babies were brought home, Pastor Osteen became very ill and went on to be with the Lord.

Although he is greatly missed, Kevin and Lisa are thankful that he was able to see God move on their behalf and bring them the children they desperately wanted. He came over to the house every day to visit with his granddaughters and be a significant part of their lives. They heard him pray over them and talk to them so much that they recognize his voice when they hear recordings of him on television, and they turn their heads to watch their grandfather preach the Word of God.

Today, the birthmother is a Bible school graduate and working full-time, as is the birthfather. While both of them miss the girls and wish they were with them, they know that the babies are better off where they are now. The young woman says that she does not regret giving the babies up because she knows who they are with and that they are well taken care of every day.

As the twins grew, God laid it on Kevin and Lisa's hearts to adopt again. In 2000, they adopted a little boy to add to their family. They now are raising three beautiful children and are serving God in everything they do. Their dreams of parenting have been fulfilled through the loving act of adoption.

Each situation and circumstance that worked to bring the fulfillment of these dreams to pass could have been seen as a separate instance, each one having nothing to do with the other. When I try to look at them from God's point of view, however, I can see how the tapestry of the lives of every person involved.

CHAPTER 8

LAURA

L aura laid across her bed with her journal open. So many thoughts were racing through her mind that she could hardly sort one out to write it down. This was different than everything she had done before—completely different, and it frightened her.

Finally she put her pen to the paper and started putting her thoughts together. "I'm more hesitant to tell her things because I know that she loves me and the Lord," she wrote, thinking about her counseling session earlier that afternoon.

Knowing that her counselor loved her brought up the fear that if she were to find out who Laura truly was, Laura would lose her approval. Surely no one could love someone as profoundly messed up as she was.

Laura was a professional patient. In the past five years, she had been through five different counselors, four psychiatrists, three nutritionists, and numerous medical doctors. Not one of them had been able to help her overcome the eating disorder that controlled her thoughts, her time, her money, and her life.

Now, suddenly, she was confronted with someone who truly cared about her and not about how much money her insurance company was going to pay. In fact, no matter how hard she tried to convince herself that they were just being nice, all the staff seemed to care about her. They did not simply focus on her behavior, but on her as a person and the reasons why she did what she did.

That meant that she was going to have to face the real issues that had been behind her struggles all along. As much as Laura wanted help, she was held back by a terrifying fear of failure. "What if I can't do it?" she thought. "What if I can't get better?"

Another voice, the voice that had prompted her to seek help and brought her to Mercy Ministries, asked her a new question.

"What if you can?"

Laura thought that her life should be perfect. Her parents loved her and they loved each other. She was smart and involved in activities that showcased her natural talents and abilities. From the outside, everything appeared right.

Inside, Laura lived in fear that she would never measure up to the standard. As the middle child of three girls, she was constantly comparing herself to her sisters. She and her oldest sister were in constant unspoken competition over their grades, and her father unknowingly added pressure to the situation by pushing them to get straight A's. Her mother was very concerned with physical fitness and had been taking Laura, who had been overweight since early childhood, to weight loss programs since the sixth grade.

All the pressure that Laura experienced began to manifest itself in depression. When she was sixteen years old, her mother took her to get help. The counselor they saw said Laura was severely depressed and needed medication, but her mother refused to start that at such a young age. Instead, they found a different counselor who put Laura in a group focused on eating disorders and depression.

That counselor thought that Laura was suicidal. She soon hospitalized her, placing her in the eating disorders unit. There Laura learned the "tricks of the trade" from the other girls, who had been practicing eating disorder behavior for years.

The hospital staff did put Laura on medication, but a few days after she came home she poured the pills down the sink. She knew she could not take the prescribed medicine and diet pills at the same time. When her parents discovered what Laura had done, they gave her an ultimatum of continuing on the medication or going back to the hospital. Unwilling to give up her diet pills, Laura went back to the hospital.

The next time she returned home, Laura simply stopped eating. She believed if she could just lose the extra pounds that plagued her, she would be happy. Telling everyone that she was a vegetarian to keep them from prying, she existed for more than six months on little more than celery sticks and coffee. She lost a hundred pounds and everybody thought it was great that she had so much willpower.

She could not continue on such a restricted diet and eventually started eating again. Terrified of gaining the weight back, she rid herself of the food by throwing up or taking massive doses of laxatives every time she ate. She discovered that purging gave her the freedom to eat and began consuming huge amounts of food.

The obsession to be thin pushed her to do things she never would have considered before. She and a friend she had met in the hospital were arrested for shoplifting laxatives. By this time, her parents had become aware that Laura's problems were far beyond the scope of what they could handle, but they did not know what else to do besides sending her to the counselor and forbidding her to see that friend. Laura never stole again, but her heart did not change. She was fundamentally unhappy with the person she was, and none of the new behaviors the counselor tried to teach her could change that.

Throughout high school, psychiatrists played with the dosage of her medication, trying to find the combination that would work for her. The problem was that Laura never knew what "normal" was supposed to feel like, so she did not necessarily know what the medication was meant to do for her. She simply called the psychiatrist every time she started feeling bad and told him that the medicine was not helping.

The invisible standard that Laura had set for herself was getting higher and higher. She was the best at everything she did, from serving as president of the Key Club to starring in the school play. She graduated first in her high school class. None of it was enough to make her feel good about herself and the depression deepened.

Laura convinced her parents that she was well enough to go away to college. She wanted to make new friends and start over in a different environment. Her parents were reluctant to let her go. Their relationship had always been extremely close and it was hard for them to imagine their daughter living so far away, especially when they knew she was sick. Even as they unpacked Laura's things in the dorm room, her mother told her they could still go home if she wanted to change her mind.

Laura hoped that a new start would help her change, but the freedom that she found at school only made things worse. She could binge in the cafeteria or bring food into her room and eat without anyone noticing. Since she had a car, she could go off campus to buy laxatives. There was no one to watch over her and she was losing more and more control.

One night, after taking about 90 laxatives, Laura blacked out in the shower. When she awoke fifteen minutes later she was lying on the floor covered in her own vomit. Her eating disorder was worse than ever. She knew she needed to get help but did not know where to turn.

When she went home for Christmas she pleaded with her counselor to find her something that would make a difference. The counselor told her that there was nothing more she could do for her. She thought hospitalization might be helpful, but in order for her to be admitted she had to be suicidal. Laura considered lying and saying she wanted to die, just to get help.

Instead, she went to a psychiatrist who was able to talk her insurance company into paying for two weeks' worth of outpatient treatment. She saw a nutritionist for the first time and was provided with a meal plan and encouraged to stay on her medication. While it was not all that Laura had hoped for, she felt that she had some kind of plan that would help her get through school.

Her unhappiness with herself was so pervasive that it began to interfere with all areas of her life. She returned for the second semester but soon realized that she did not want to stay at school. The program she was studying did not meet her standards, and she thought she would be better off somewhere else. She moved back home.

One good thing that had come out of Laura's year away at school was that her relationship with God had grown stronger. She had attended church with her parents for most of her life, and in the tenth grade had asked Jesus into her heart to be her personal Lord and Savior. Since then, however, there had not been anyone to teach her how to take the head knowledge that she had about God and translate it into heart knowledge that would change her life.

Laura had become involved with a campus ministry that helped her grow spiritually. She had also found a church where she was comfortable. Still, even in those circles, it seemed that no one knew how to help her. They would direct her to good books about her struggles, but Laura already knew what most of the books said. The problem for her was in applying the information to her life.

Even though she did not find much specific help, Laura realized that the answers she was seeking were going to somehow be found through her relationship with God. Her parents were glad she had found something that she needed at church while away at school, and they let her find one she was comfortable with at home rather than making her attend with them.

Laura enrolled in a college that was four minutes away from home but she lived on campus. Although she had switched environments once again, her problems had followed her. Her second year was more of the same—going to class, working, and spending all her money and free time on food. She continued going to church, but even that had become routine. Counseling was not helping her and she quit that altogether.

During that year and the next, Laura became sicker and sicker. She constantly binged and purged, throwing up ten to twelve times a day and using 30-60 laxatives at once. Her thoughts were completely consumed by food. Instead of taking notes in class, Laura spent her time figuring out what she wanted to eat and how much she could buy with the money she had left. She was almost always broke because of junk food binges. When her roommate went home on the weekends,

Laura took the phone off the hook so she could concentrate on eating. She had no life other than food.

After an extreme binge, Laura was in such severe pain that she called 911 from her dorm room. She thought she had taken so many laxatives that her stomach was exploding. The truth was that it was her heart that was causing the distress. The laxative abuse had lowered her potassium to a dangerous level.

Laura was forced to start counseling again following that incident. She found a counselor who specialized in eating disorders and was referred to a nutritionist. She also started seeing a psychiatrist again. None of it helped. The obsession with being thin and her desire for perfection so overwhelmed her that none of their suggestions worked. Everything they offered dealt with her behavior—follow a meal plan, make a list of three other things to do instead of purging, plan to binge once a week. Laura believes now that she probably could have stopped the behavior but would have most likely have switched to something else because the root had not been addressed.

Her counselor and psychiatrist had often tried to pinpoint the root of Laura's problems, but they had been unsuccessful. They probed into her background, finding nothing that would suggest what had triggered the eating disorder. Her parents were still together, Laura had never been abused, and no other warning signs appeared as they discussed her life. Since they could not point to a justifiable reason for her behavior, Laura started to believe there must be something fundamentally wrong with her as a person.

By the end of that school year, Laura was so depressed that she could not get out of bed. She stopped going to class. She almost stopped functioning altogether. Before final exams started, she left and went home. It was simply too painful to deal with what her life had become, and she called her counselor to say that she was going to kill herself.

The truth was that she did not want to die. She just wanted help. She was tired of trying again and again only to fail every time. Her counselor talked her into going to the emergency room. When Laura arrived there, she was clearly suicidal. In spite of the fact that the situation was obviously serious and that it was 2 a.m., someone from her insurance company had to be called to make sure she was sick enough to be admitted.

Laura stayed in the hospital for two days, although she told them she would kill herself if they let her go home. When they released her, she went home, took two bottles of pills, and went to her counselor's office for her appointment. She told her she had just come to say goodbye. The counselor called 911 immediately.

Following that incident, Laura participated in an outpatient treatment program for a month where they did little more than play around with her medication, trying to find the right dosage and combination. By this time she was on serious drugs, including Lithium and Prozac, and they caused her to shake all day long.

Just a few days before the new semester started, Laura decided to go back to the school she had gone to for her first year. She thought the problem was that she had picked the wrong major and that she really did not want to be in education. She switched to computer science. Within a week, she found an apartment and a roommate and enrolled in classes.

She remembers very little of that time, except for what her roommate has told her. Her roommate, a girl Laura had met in the hospital, used to walk into the apartment and find Laura sitting in the living room with food spread out everywhere around her. Laura would buy food and her roommate would throw it out. When she tried to suggest that Laura would be better off at home, Laura told her that the only way she was going home was in a body bag.

Things got bad enough by Thanksgiving that Laura did go home. She decided to switch doctors again. Since she was still sick, she assumed the last doctor did not know any more than the others had. There was always a place outside of herself that Laura could lay the blame—it was the school's fault, or the doctor's, or the counselor's.

Her nutritionist worked in an outpatient program that she thought might help, and she referred Laura to a new doctor in order to be assessed and checked in. Laura immediately told this doctor that she was planning to drive her car off an overpass. This got her admitted to the hospital for the third time. She had sabotaged herself, fearing that the new program would not help her any more than the others had. Laura was too weak to face the reality of failure once again.

After they changed her medication once more and sent her home, she overdosed again. She was rushed to the emergency room where her stomach was pumped. They sent her to intensive care and then into the psychiatric ward. Although Laura wanted to be admitted to an eating disorder hospital, the insurance company would not pay for it unless she was medically compromised. The only focus of her treatment was alleviating the depression so that she could go home. Throughout her hospital stay she either refused to eat or threw up what she was forced to consume.

The doctor told Laura she needed to accept the fact that this was something totally beyond her control. Her body was messed up and she needed to be on medication for the rest of her life. Laura truly resented that. One of her desires was to be off all the medication. At the end of his rope, the doctor offered shock therapy as one last option to treat the depression.

Laura underwent five ECT treatments. Most of that time is sketchy in her memory now, a side effect of the shock therapy. She does remember spending a few days in the state hospital afterwards. That was the worst experience of her life. Surrounded by severe schizophrenics and people who constantly needed shots to quiet their outbursts, Laura did nothing but cry. She pulled it together enough to write out a plan for what she would do if she got depressed again, and the hospital released her in time for Christmas.

It turned out to be a good Christmas. It seemed the shock therapy had helped the depression, although it had not affected the eating disorder. She continued meeting with her counselor, whom she had been seeing for the last two and a half years, and she attended groups for eating disorders and depression.

By January, Laura felt she was stable enough on her medication to return to school. Until then, Laura had tried to hide her eating disorder from every college roommate she had, believing that they would either interfere with her plans or reject her because of her behavior. None of her previous roommates had noticed, or if they had, they had not said anything to Laura about it. This time, she had a Christian roommate who truly cared about her. She knew that Laura was severely bulimic and confronted her. They both cried as Laura was finally honest about wanting help but not knowing where to turn.

That spring, a friend called Laura and told her that she had a brochure about a place called Mercy Ministries that she wanted her to see. Laura had been to a Point of Grace concert and heard about Mercy Ministries before, but it had never crossed her mind that it would be something she would need. She had never thought she would let herself get in as deep as she now had.

It was as if something clicked inside Laura and she knew that this was what she needed to do. She had goals and dreams for her life, and she would never survive if she continued on this path. She wanted to get off her medication and move on with her life. Somehow, she knew Mercy Ministries was the place that would teach her how to apply all the things she knew about God to her life so that she could be set free from her eating disorder forever.

When Laura told her counselor that she was applying to this program, she was stunned by her response. She was very angry that Laura would pursue that type of treatment, insisting that it was impossible to be set free from an eating disorder. While it might be possible for Laura to get better, she would always be in recovery. Her counselor insisted that an eating disorder was something Laura would have to deal with for the rest of her life.

Laura was hurt by the reaction, but not swayed. Even though her counselor gave her an ultimatum about choosing between meeting with her and applying to Mercy, Laura chose to proceed with her application. It was a tough decision. That counselor had been more of a friend to Laura than some of her friends had been. Still, Laura realized that it was time to start depending on God instead of people.

It took her a long time after arriving at Mercy to accept that the staff truly cared about her. She thought she had been fooling everyone her whole life, making them believe she was smart when she was really stupid. She felt completely worthless and unsalvageable. If people were nice to her she thought they either felt sorry for her or that she had pulled the wool over their eyes.

Once she started to believe that the staff's concern for her was genuine, she became frightened. If their love for her was real, she ran the risk of losing it when they found out who she truly was. Her fear of failure kicked into overdrive at the thought of that possibility.

Slowly but surely, however, Laura began to learn the truth. She discovered that God had been willing to sacrifice His Son, Jesus, for her (John 3:16). That was a fact that Laura had always known, and she had already accepted Christ's death on the cross as payment for her sins. What was revelation to her was that the motivation behind God's gift of salvation was His incredible love. For the first time, Laura began to understand that if God loved her so much, she must be someone who was worth loving.

When she started to believe that God truly loved her, people's opinions of her began to matter less and less. It was okay if someone did not like her, or if she did not measure up to someone else's standard, because she was fully loved, completely accepted, and totally pleasing to God. She learned to become a God-pleaser rather than a man-pleaser (Galatians 1:10). That set her free from the need to strive for perfection.

A major barrier in Laura's relationship with God came crashing down one afternoon as she sat by herself in the classroom, reading her Bible. Because of the long process that she had gone through in seeking help from secular institutions and the number of times that she had been disappointed, she struggled with believing that God could truly heal her. It was a trust issue and it ran deep in Laura's heart.

As she read 1 Corinthians 1:9 (CEV), the words seemed to leap off of the page. ***God can be trusted, and he chose you to be partners with his Son, our Lord Jesus Christ.*** She had to read it two or three times before she believed that her eyes were not playing tricks on her. There it was, written right there on the page, especially for her. ***God can be trusted!*** That one moment solidified it for Laura. God was worthy of her trust and she placed it in Him.

Laura took every one of the Scriptures that her counselor gave her about her identity in Christ and looked them up in different versions of the Bible. When she found the one that fit her best, she wrote it down and kept it where she could read it whenever she began to doubt who she truly was. All of the truths that she had known in her head were finally becoming real in her heart.

She learned that God had created her in His image. According to Psalm 139, He had created her inmost being, knitting her together in her mother's womb, and she was fearfully and wonderfully made. Not only had God created her, but He also had a purpose for her. Jeremiah 29:11 told her that His plan was to prosper and not to harm her, to give her hope and a future. There was something out there that God intended for her to do, and she became determined to discover what that was.

Healing came in every area of Laura's life during the six months she spent at Mercy Ministries. Although she had lived a normal childhood, there had been things that happened in her life which were very hurtful. When she had talked to her previous counselors about those issues, it felt like all they did was talk. There was no healing.

When her counselor at Mercy encouraged her to pour her heart out before the Lord as David did in Psalm 142:2, she found that He was able to remove the pain from her memory so that it no longer hurt when she recalled it. She discovered that He truly was the God who could heal her (Exodus 15:26). A few months into her stay, Laura was completely free from the medication she had depended on for so long.

Even though she was learning to replace the false beliefs she had held about herself with the truth of the Word, Laura still struggled with bulimia. The behaviors had become very much a habit, and as much as she did not want to engage in them any longer, she sometimes did. She learned to constantly pray for strength and to call on the verses that she was memorizing to get her through the toughest temptations.

The key to Laura's freedom, she believes, was in experiencing unconditional love. It was the first time that she did not feel the pressure to perform in order to be accepted. She did not have to be perfect because she was loved simply for who she was, mistakes and all. In time, she came to understand that the staff loved her that way because of the love of God that they experienced in their own lives. When she accepted that love for herself, she was able to begin giving it to others as well.

When she graduated from Mercy Ministries, Laura returned home and worked until school started again. At first there seemed to be a "honeymoon period" when everything was great. However, Laura's life has not been free from difficulty since then. She continues to struggle with temptation and she has stumbled.

What she found out, however, was that when she opened the door to Satan's influence in that part of her life, everything else fell apart— her job, finances, school. She had to learn to repent, acknowledge that she had messed up, turn her back on the sin, and move on.

A mistake did not mean that she was bulimic again. It was simply a mistake. She responded to the gentle conviction of the Holy Spirit, who guides us into all truth (John 16:13), rather than falling under the harsh condemnation of Satan, who is the accuser of the brethren (Revelation 12:10). In that way, she was able to continue walking in the healing and the freedom that God had brought about in her life.

Today, Laura no longer faces those struggles. She found a healthy balance, eating food that she likes when she is hungry, but only enough of it to satisfy her physical needs. At one point, she even worked in a restaurant, and the constant exposure to food was not an issue for her.

Laura completed her bachelor's degree in Elementary and Special Education in May of 2000. She contacted me then about working for Mercy Ministries, and I told her that we did not have any jobs available, but that I would keep her in mind if anything opened up. Laura, with a great amount of determination, decided to return to school and completed her Master's Degree in Education and even wrote her thesis on eating disorders! At the same time, our Director of Education was leaving and Laura immediately moved to Nashville and began working in our home there.

Now Laura is an important part of the Mercy Ministries team, working with the girls and also in the corporate office. She also speaks often, sharing her testimony of overcoming an eating disorder. She has a unique ability to minister to the girls who come to our homes and are suffering from the devastation of eating disorders. Every day I see her at work, I am amazed at the transformation that has taken place!

CHAPTER 9

KELLY

"I've had enough of this!" Kelly told her roommate. "I'm tired of him controlling my life. He has my car keys, my meal card, all of my money. He won't even let me go to the mall with you because he's convinced that I'll talk to guys there. This is ridiculous. I'm breaking up with him, today."

She called her boyfriend and he came over to meet her outside the girls' dorm. Together they walked toward the courtyard on campus. Kelly thought it would be safe to tell him her decision in a public place. He would not dare hurt her in front of so many witnesses.

As they sat down, Kelly drew in a deep breath. "I can't do this anymore," she told him. "It's over."

For a moment he stared at her in silent disbelief. Then he exploded in a rage like Kelly had never seen before. He tore his shirt in half and screamed that he was going to kill himself. In shock and amazement, Kelly watched as he ran and smashed his head into a brick wall.

"Okay!" she cried. "Okay, stop! I didn't mean it. I'm sorry. I'm not breaking up with you."

Kelly stayed in that relationship for almost two years. Every time she wanted to get away, it seemed that something drew her back and kept her entangled. He threatened suicide until she decided she no longer cared if he killed himself. Then he threatened to kill her.

Kelly had grown up in a strong Christian home. Her parents were in the ministry and had traveled the country from the time Kelly was three or four years old. As a child, she had a tender heart for the Lord and was used by God to minister to many people.

Her parents' lifestyle kept them in constant contact with ministers from around the world. Time and again, Kelly was told that one day she would go into the ministry herself with the great man of God she was to marry. Kelly believed that was God's plan for her life and kept that dream in her heart as she grew up.

When she became a teenager, however, Kelly's life began to change. She became tired of being a preacher's kid. She started growing cold towards the things of God and the dream in her heart began to fade away. Powerful church services no longer captivated her attention. She was usually bored, wondering when they would be over so she could go home.

During this time, Kelly's parents decided to take her out of private school and put her into the public school system. This happened during the beginning of her ninth grade year. Until that point, Kelly had led a very sheltered life and her parents felt she might be missing out on important opportunities. Although they wanted her to be exposed to new and different things, they did not expect Kelly to involve herself quite as she did.

That year, Kelly attended a New Year's Eve party with a friend who had grown up in church with her. The two girls were at the same point in their relationship with the Lord, distracted by the things of the world and disinterested in the things of God. It was at that party that Kelly experimented with alcohol for the first time. She found she naturally had a very high tolerance for it and was able to consume a great deal. She drank heavily that night and alcohol quickly became a habit.

A pattern was established in Kelly's life. She could not let her parents know about her drinking so she began lying about where she was going, whom she was with, and what they would be doing. She began dating, mostly older boys who were involved in the party scene and kept her supplied with alcohol.

Although her parents suspected that something was wrong, Kelly always seemed to have a good excuse or a valid reason to explain her behavior. Wanting to believe the best about their daughter, they chose to accept what she said as the truth. Kelly lived this double life throughout high school, partying with her friends and lying to her family to convince them everything was fine.

During her junior year, Kelly's boyfriend asked her to the senior party and she accepted. They attended a pre-party at a friend's house. There was a barrel filled with what appeared to be red Kool-Aid on the back lawn. Kelly began drinking it and eventually found herself leaning so far over the edge of the barrel to get another cupful that her arm was stained red halfway to her shoulder.

The Kool-Aid turned out to be Jungle Juice, a highly alcoholic drink. A very intoxicated Kelly arrived at the senior party, where she ran into an old boyfriend of hers. He was a young man who had always been close friends with Kelly's family. When he realized what was happening with Kelly, he became very concerned for her. He decided to go to her parents and inform them of the choices she had been making.

Confronted with the truth from a young man they trusted, Kelly's parents could no longer deny the fact that Kelly was in trouble. They decided to send her to California to live with her older sister for the summer, hoping that time away from her environment and friends would help her make better choices. For a time, it seemed to work. Kelly stopped drinking and made the kind of progress, at least outwardly, that her family was hoping to see.

When Kelly returned to begin her senior year of high school, her parents sent her back to a private school. They again hoped that a different environment would keep her out of trouble. Unfortunately, it was Kelly's desire to be in trouble and she quickly gravitated to the same kind of friends as before.

She started going to nightclubs, lying to her parents about where she would be so she could spend the evening dancing and drinking. A normal night for Kelly included drinking a pint of Bacardi on the way to a club and then twelve shots of Jaegermeister or four Long Island Iced Teas while there.

During this time, Kelly continued attending church with her family, mostly for the sake of keeping up appearances. At a youth service one night, a friend of her parents who was in the ministry called Kelly out from the pew and told her that if she did not change her life, she would die. The words hardly had an impact on Kelly. All she could think was, "Please don't tell my mom." She refused to change.

The web of lies that Kelly was weaving became more and more complex. Several times she almost got caught. One day her mother answered the phone at their home and discovered that the caller was an employee of a nightclub in town. He was calling to say that they had found Kelly's driver's license in the parking lot and that she could come in to pick it up any time. When confronted about the call, Kelly assured her mother that she had not been in the nightclub, but at a comedy club across the parking lot instead. Somehow, Kelly was able to convince her mother that she was telling the truth.

Eventually Kelly graduated from high school and decided to move away and try things on her own. She got an apartment with a friend, found a good job, and even started going to church again. She stopped drinking and it seemed like her life was straightening out. Then she and her roommate began having problems and Kelly returned home.

Soon after, Kelly was back to her old pattern. One night at a club, Kelly ran into a boy, Steven, whom she had known since kindergarten. He called her house the next day and Kelly's mother took the message since Kelly was not home. When her mother told her that he had called, she also told her that she had a bad feeling about him and asked Kelly to please not call him back. Although Kelly had not intended to return the call, her rebellion had become so strong that her mother's request not to call was the only reason that she did.

Steven was a very outgoing and likable young man and they began dating. Both he and Kelly drank heavily, and Steven introduced her to the drug Ecstasy. At first they would use it about once a week. Then it increased to four times a week. Soon they were using it twice a night, four times a week, often fighting over the bigger half of a split pill when it was the only one left.

Kelly began to see another side of Steven, one that was jealous and controlling and sometimes explosive. He began imagining that she was talking to guys on her way to the bathroom so he would walk her there and wait outside the door until she emerged. They were always together and it was always on Steven's terms.

Finally, Kelly's parents told her not to see him anymore. She had seen enough to make her think about getting out of the relationship, but with her parents pushing her, the rebellion in her again pushed back. Instead of following her instincts, she began lying to her parents and sneaking around to be with him.

Kelly had planned to go away to school that fall, to a college different than the one Steven would be attending. He convinced her to switch schools so they could be together, telling her that once they were away from her parents' watchful eyes, their relationship would be so much better.

However, being away from home actually meant that Steven could control even more of Kelly's life. He went with her to register for classes and would not let her take any classes without him. He took her car keys away from her and kept her meal card so that she could not eat without him. He held her mailbox keys so that any time she got a letter with money inside, he could keep it for her. She was forced to be with him all the time.

The same rebellion that had caused Kelly to go against her parents began rising up against Steven. She tried to go out with her girlfriends, but he always tracked her down. Several times she tried to break up with him, but he consistently found a way to draw her back. One time he made such a scene outside her dorm that her suitemates asked her to go talk to him, just so he would shut up long enough for them to study. Every time he felt her slipping away, he would threaten to kill himself. Kelly gave in to him every time.

Steven crossed the line at a club one night. He and Kelly were outside in the parking lot, involved in a heated argument, when he yanked a ring off of Kelly's hand and threw it into a nearby field. Kelly became so angry with him that she ran back into the club and told the bodyguards that he was trying to attack her. They prevented him from entering the club while she stayed inside and danced with her friends, enjoying her first time away from him in months.

One of the bodyguards stayed with her, just to be sure. It turned out to be a wise precaution because Steven managed to get back into the club after paying someone in the parking lot to switch shirts with him. He came after Kelly. The bodyguard threw him down and they fought. Steven was arrested.

Kelly thought for sure that she had made a clean break from him this time. Then his mother called and told her that Steven was running up and down the streets, screaming for Kelly and that no one else could calm him down. She begged Kelly to come and pick him up. Once again Kelly gave in. Taking a friend with her for protection, she went and picked him up. He was calm, and although Kelly could tell he was extremely high, he seemed truly repentant for the things he had done to hurt her.

Somehow he convinced Kelly to drop her friend off and drive back to school alone with him. Once her friend was out of the car, he became angry again and began yelling at her and punching the dashboard. One of his punches shut off all of the digital instruments on Kelly's dashboard. Frightened and angry, Kelly pulled over and kicked him out of the car.

Kelly got back to her dorm room and her phone was already ringing. It was Steven, calling from a pay phone, sobbing. Guilt took over and she went back to pick him up. The next day she tried again to break up with him, but the same scene replayed itself, as always. He threatened to kill himself and she backed down. That cycle occurred again and again throughout their relationship.

The final straw for Kelly came when she decided to rush a Christian sorority on campus. Since he could not be a part of it, he would not let her join. At that point, Kelly decided that she was definitely ending the relationship, no matter what he said or did. If he wanted to kill himself, she would let him. It was more important to her to be free from his domination of her life.

She went to his room to talk to him. Steven was surprisingly calm when he heard her say that she was breaking up with him, once and for all. He said that he understood and that he knew he had not treated her like she deserved to be treated. Amazed, Kelly began to feel a burden lifting from her shoulders.

Suddenly everything went into slow motion. Kelly watched as Steven picked up a huge steak knife and held it up over his head. She heard him say that if he could not have her, then no one would. He would kill her first and then himself. Scrambling to get away from him, Kelly fell backwards onto the floor and lay there, frozen. All she could think was, "At least I'll be free." She saw the knife come down, and waited for pain that never came.

Instead of stabbing her, Steven plunged the knife into his own forearm and immediately began screaming in agony. Terrified, Kelly drove him to the emergency room, where he made up a story about slipping with the knife and cutting himself by accident. On the way home, he was so angry with Kelly because he was hurt that he smashed his head into her windshield and shattered it.

Kelly was at a loss. She no longer had any idea what to do or how to get out of the situation. It was about that time that she had a dream about a baby girl trying to jump into a pool of water. She knew instantly that she was pregnant with a little girl. She told Steven, who was excited and wanted to get married. Kelly knew that was not what she wanted. She did not want to be trapped in this relationship any more. Once again, she searched for a way out.

Finally she called and confessed everything to her parents, who had no idea that they were even at the same school, let alone involved in any type of relationship. They came to school to see her and took her to the police station. For months Steven had been setting Kelly up, taking things from his parents' home each time they visited there together so that it would look like Kelly had stolen them. His mother had called Kelly's parents and threatened to have her arrested.

Kelly's parents knew that if they did not present her with some difficult choices, she might end up right back where she had been. As hard as it was for them to do, they took a firm stand with her. They talked to her while they sat at the police station, and told her she could either choose to go home with them or stay in jail.

Kelly chose to leave with them. They went back to her room and packed her things. Even then, Kelly tried to manipulate them into letting her stay by telling them she had finals she could not miss or by making up some other reason why she could not leave. Her parents stood firm, reminding her that her only other option was to return to the police station.

As they walked out to load Kelly's things into the car, Steven appeared. He was too afraid of Kelly's father to approach, so he drove around them in circles, yelling, "What about the baby? What about the baby?"

"What is he saying?" Kelly's mom asked her.

"Oh, I don't know," Kelly said, dismissing it with a wave of her hand. "He's just calling me baby." She was not prepared to tell her parents that she was pregnant with his child.

They drove away, but Steven followed them home. Several times over the weekend Kelly's parents moved her around to different places to protect her, but he always managed to find her. Finally the decision was made that Kelly would come to the Mercy Ministries home in West Monroe, Louisiana.

Kelly's parents were long time friends of mine and her mother had often visited the program to minister to the girls there. I had been aware of the situation with Kelly for some time and had been providing counsel to her parents. Now that Kelly herself appeared to want help, I knew it was time to bring her in.

No one except Kelly and Steven knew about her pregnancy. Kelly herself was living in complete denial of the fact. She wrote on her application that she was not pregnant and told no one at Mercy Ministries that she even suspected she might be. Terribly ill, the work details and the cooking that she was required to do as a resident of the home took all of her effort. She was constantly throwing up and lost sixteen pounds in four months.

The staff believed Kelly when she said she was suffering from drug withdrawals, until her illness became so severe they had to take her to the hospital. While there, Kelly had an ultrasound. No longer able to deny the truth, Kelly accepted the fact that she was pregnant. Her first thought as she laid there looking at the screen was that every preacher who had ever told her how happy her life would be and what an incredible man of God she would marry had just been proven wrong. Her life was ruined and her dreams were dead.

Kelly had already learned a great deal as a result of being in the program, despite her constant illness. She realized that the reason she was always drawn back to Steven and could not let go, despite his abusiveness, was the result of a soul tie. In his book, *Seductions Exposed*, which every girl who comes into Mercy Ministries is required to read, Gary Greenwald describes a soul tie as "the knitting together of two souls that can either bring tremendous blessings in a godly relationship or tremendous destruction when made with the wrong person."

The physical and emotional bond between Kelly and Steven had become so strong that the most intimate parts of themselves, their souls, were joined. That soul tie enabled Steven to manipulate and abuse Kelly because her mind, will, and emotions were open to him. Kelly's counselor led her through the process of breaking that soul tie and any other ties that might be holding her back. She worked through forgiving Steven, releasing him from having any power over her. Slowly, God restored things in Kelly's life that the enemy had stolen from her.

Still, in spite of the healing that Kelly recognized in her life, she was not yet totally committed to changing. She was constantly thinking about running away. She hated being on someone else's time schedule and under someone else's rules. When Christmas break came and Kelly went home for two weeks, she made her choice.

Unfortunately, Kelly chose to re-establish the soul tie with Steven that she had previously broken. She convinced herself that he was the only person who could understand her. In the middle of the night, she ran away and went back to him. They moved hundreds of miles away to live with his sister.

Within a month, Kelly realized that she had made a mistake. Steven and his sister were heavily involved in drugs, moving on from the things Kelly had once done with him to harder drugs like cocaine, crystal, and acid. She knew she did not want to raise her child in that environment so she called missionary friends of her parents who lived in the area to pick her up. She returned to her parents' house soon after. The last thing she ever heard about Steven was that he had been rushed to the hospital due to a drug overdose.

There were no options left for Kelly. Her relationship with her family was severely damaged. She had lost all of her friends and her chance at a college education. With nothing left, Kelly turned back to God.

This time she was determined to change her life and be a good mother to the child who was about to enter the world. Her early upbringing and her time at Mercy Ministries had taught her that the only way to get her life completely straightened out was to give it over to God. From the day she made the decision to turn her heart completely to the Lord, He began working in her life.

Kelly's sister offered to let her come and live with her family in another state. Her parents wanted her to return to Mercy Ministries, but Kelly did not feel that was the right thing for her to do at the time. I agreed that living with her sister was the best option for Kelly. Already seven months pregnant, Kelly moved and started her new life.

Things changed rapidly. Kelly started going to church again and God continued to work in her heart, changing her from the inside out. One night, in a dream, God told her to call the pastor. She called and made an appointment with him without knowing why she was supposed to talk to him.

They sat down together and discussed Kelly's situation. With just two weeks to go before her due date, the challenges she was about to face were obvious. The pastor asked her what she was planning to do to support herself and the baby, and Kelly replied that she did not yet know.

The pastor told her that he had an opening for a secretary to the assistant pastor, children's pastor, and youth pastor. Kelly was interviewed on the spot and given the job. She was to start as soon as the baby was born.

At first, Kelly struggled with feelings of unworthiness. She did not think that she deserved to be blessed in the way that God was blessing her because she had turned against Him and made poor choices. Despite her feelings, however, she worked hard and continued to seek out the will of God for her life.

Kelly was unaware that while she prayed and asked God for His perfect plan in her life, the youth pastor she was working for was also praying. Kevin was praying for a wife, and he asked God to put her right under his nose so he would not miss her.

They became friends as Kelly helped out with the youth group. After about a year, he called and asked her out. It was evident that Kevin had great respect for Kelly and that was something she never thought she would receive from anyone again. Because Kevin thought she had worth and value, Kelly began to realize that God thought of her in the same way. Her opinion of herself began to change as well. They dated for about a year.

While they were dating, Kelly's daughter, Kelsi, was growing up quickly. Kelly had asked God to bring Kelsi a daddy by the time she was two years old. Although she had not mentioned it to many people, and certainly not to Kelsi, Kelly was beginning to believe that Kevin might be the man God had chosen to fulfill that role.

You can imagine her surprise when Kelsi, completely out of the blue, looked up at Kevin one day and called him "Daddy." Kelly was frozen, not knowing how to respond or even whether she should respond at all.

She did not want Kevin to think that she had encouraged Kelsi to see him in that role, nor did she want to publicly discourage her daughter and cause Kevin to believe she was not interested in him as a future husband and father. Unsure of how to react, Kelly let the moment pass without saying anything about it.

However, Kevin had already been considering the possibility of becoming Kelsi's daddy, and he believed that it was a part of God's plan for them. Just before Kelsi's second birthday, Kevin made the unofficial title of "daddy" that Kelsi had given him official.

He received permission from the senior pastor to have a few moments on the platform during a special Father's Day worship service to which he had invited both his and Kelly's families. With tears in his eyes, Kevin spoke of his life-long desire to marry his best friend. Kelly had no idea what was happening, but as he began to walk down the aisle toward her, it dawned on her that something special was taking place. In front of the entire church, Kevin got down on one knee, professed his love to Kelly, and asked her to marry him. Kelly was stunned but thrilled to accept his marriage proposal.

After they married, Kevin legally adopted Kelsi. Their precious family has grown since then with the addition of three more beautiful daughters. Today, Kevin is the pastor of his own congregation and Kelly serves alongside him in the ministry. The dreams from long ago that she had once thought were impossible to achieve have all come to pass in her life.

Looking back on her life now, Kelly can see how many times God gave her an opportunity to stop the destructive patterns that she had set for herself. There were so many warning signs: the ex-boyfriend who told her parents about her drinking; the friend of her parents who told her she had to change or she would die; the time she dropped her license in the parking lot of the club. At any one of those moments, she could have stopped. Each time was a chance to admit her struggles, ask for help, and let God take control of her life again.

Still, although she ignored God's hand in her life so many times, she knows beyond the shadow of a doubt that He heard the cry of her heart the moment she turned back to Him. From that second, He has worked in her life to do things that were beyond her wildest imagination. God has restored all of her dreams. He has not brought her back quietly, but rewarded her openly for the choices she made as she sought out what He would have her do with her life.

Kelly's mother still travels in the ministry and often comes to the Mercy Ministries homes to minister to the girls. Recently, Kelly began accompanying her mother on her trips so that she could share her testimony. It is so powerful for the residents to hear both sides of the story—a parent and a former resident. As they tag-team preach, they are able to open many of the girls' eyes to what their own parents may be going through even as they are trying to get their lives together in the program. For many of them, it is the first time they are able to understand their parents' point of view.

When Kelly stands before the girls in the home and speaks, she has their complete attention. She tells the girls that she once was where they are. She tried everything worldly to find happiness and it only led to emptiness. She knows that if God can work the miracles in her life that have already come to pass, He can do the same for them.

The girls hang on Kelly's every word because they can see in her eyes that she understands them and is speaking the truth. They know that right in front of them is a living example of God's power. When they hear her story they remember the dreams that were in their hearts long ago, the dreams that many of them have let die, and they begin to rekindle the flame beneath them.

Suddenly the girls understand that the choices they made, while they have serious consequences, have not ruined their lives or canceled the plans that God has for them. Romans 11:29 says, *the gifts and calling of God are without repentance.* That means that although we may make serious errors or a number of bad choices, God does not change His mind about the things He has planned for us to do.

Instead, God is able to use the things that we have gone through to reach out to others, just as Kelly reaches out to the people of her congregation and to the girls in the Mercy Ministries homes. She brings a message of forgiveness, hope, and mercy, and encourages them to apply it to their own lives. In turn, they will carry the same message to countless others.

CHAPTER 10

LISA

L isa sat on the front porch steps of her house, her elbows resting on her knees and her chin in her hands. A steady rain was falling and the chill in the air bit through her light jacket. Still, she knew it was useless to knock on the door and ask if she could come inside.

"Stay out there and be quiet," her mother would say. "Your father's not home yet and I don't want to deal with you." The door would be shut firmly in her face, as it had been many times before.

She knew she was being punished for something, but it had been going on so long that Lisa could not remember what it was that she had done. Her mother, however, always seemed to remember such things—for a very long time.

Later, after her parents and brother had eaten dinner, Lisa was finally allowed inside the house. There was a plate waiting for her on the table. She sat down under the watchful eye of her mother, who wanted to be sure that Lisa did not steal any extra food. Lisa knew that when she finished, she would have to wash the family's dishes and then go straight to bed.

She sighed and began to eat. At least tonight she was allowed to have dinner.

Looking at Lisa today as she walks across a spacious campus, laughing and talking animatedly with friends as they head for their next class, you would think that she is just a normal college student. She is a bright girl, full of potential, with big dreams. You could not know the kind of life she lived before.

You might not ever know, unless you were to ask her about her family. Then you might see her eyes cloud over and sadness touch her face. She would tell you that she does not talk to them much these days. At nineteen, she is pretty much on her own, making her way in the world without their help. For a young woman, Lisa has already had to do a lot of that.

When she was eighteen months old, Lisa was found abandoned on the steps of a police station in another country. She was placed in an orphanage. Her earliest memories are only of darkness, accompanied by a pervasive sense of fear. While she does not necessarily remember the reasons for that fear, she knows that it controlled her life for a very long time.

An American couple adopted Lisa at the age of two, after she had been in the orphanage for six months. When she arrived in the United States, Lisa was malnourished and scarred by numerous cigarette burns. She reacted in fear at the sight of any kind of belt or rope. It was obvious that she had been badly abused.

The abuse left more than physical scars on Lisa. Her emotions were severely damaged as well. From the beginning, she was distrustful of her adoptive parents and extremely uncomfortable around them. They would leave toys on bottom shelves in the living room for Lisa to play with, but she would not touch them while her parents were in the room. If they left her alone, she would take them out and play like a normal child. The moment her parents returned, however, she put them back and became instantly quiet.

Lisa's parents were sorely disappointed in the lack of a connection that they felt with her. Although they were physically able to have children, they had chosen to adopt because they believed it was an act of service to God to care for an underprivileged child. The difficulties with Lisa caused resentment and hurt feelings, and they did not know how to handle that.

When Lisa was five years old, her parents completed a second international adoption, bringing home a little boy. Gerald was just a few months younger than Lisa. At first Lisa was thrilled to have a brother. She had asked for a brother for Christmas! Soon after he arrived, Lisa's feelings began to change. It was clear that Gerald was the favorite. She felt as if she was being pushed aside and squeezed out of the family.

Throughout elementary school, Lisa refused to do her homework. She consistently disobeyed her teachers and spent a great deal of time in detention and in-school suspension. The distrust she had for her parents spilled over into disrespect for all authority figures in her life. Getting in trouble seemed to be the only way to get her parents' attention.

From the time that her parents adopted Gerald, Lisa had been in therapy. She would see one psychiatrist for a while, and then her parents would decide they did not like that therapist and transfer her to a new one. There was little progress made with any of them because Lisa felt they all sided with her parents rather than trying to see things from her point of view. She emotionally shut down and refused to share information during her sessions. That led to diagnoses of everything from attention deficit disorder to oppositional defiant disorder to multiple personality disorder.

Lisa's parents, especially her mother, began to see everything she did as a deliberate attempt to hurt them. While there were times that Lisa was so angry that she did want to hurt them, most of her behavior was a desperate cry for attention. They responded by punishing her. She was made to clean the house or rake the yard by herself when she was just eleven or twelve years old. Often she was locked out of the house or denied meals.

Sometimes, when she was not allowed to eat, Lisa would sneak into the kitchen and steal food. That horrified her mother and caused her to punish Lisa more severely. In the sixth grade, Lisa began stealing money from her mother's friend who drove her to school each morning, using it to buy food from the cafeteria.

When the woman realized that Lisa was stealing from her, she told Lisa's mother. After ranting and raving about the shame and embarrassment that Lisa had brought upon the family, Lisa's mother banished her to the front porch as she had many times before. This time, however, as Lisa went outside, her mother told her that she never wanted to see her again. Lisa believed her and ran away.

Four hours later, the police found Lisa walking down the highway. She did not have any idea where she was going; she only knew that her mother never wanted to see her again. She knew she needed to go somewhere other than home. The police took her back to the station and called her parents. When her mother arrived, she grabbed Lisa without a word and took her home, where she promptly locked her in her room.

Lisa's father was the only one to tell her that he was glad she was home. He had always been good to her, but only when his wife was not around. She controlled him by threatening to leave anytime he disagreed with her, especially over her treatment of Lisa. The one time that he stood up to her, saying that she was overreacting in punishing Lisa, she had packed her bags and left for several days. Since then, his support of Lisa had been subtle, hidden, and much less than what she desired or needed.

Lisa lived in fear of displeasing her mother. Underneath all the anger that had built up over the years of constant rejection, there was a little girl who truly wanted her mother's love. She believed that her mother didn't want her because she was not good enough to be her daughter. Every time she was shunned or pushed away, that belief was reinforced and the hurt went deeper.

Sometimes the pain went beyond emotional and psychological to physical. Although her mother rarely left visible marks, she often slapped Lisa or pulled her hair or shoved her up against walls. One time she did leave a bruise on Lisa's hand by hitting her with a wooden spoon so hard that it broke. Lisa told a guidance counselor what had happened and that her parents deprived her of meals and locked her out of the house. He called her parents. Lisa's mother wove a web of deceit strong enough to convince the counselor that Lisa was a liar and nothing she said could be believed. Lisa did not bother trying to tell anyone again.

Life at home deteriorated to the point where all Lisa did was fight with her parents. She started lying when she got in trouble because she was afraid of the consequences. Her mother told her that if she would just tell the truth, she would be better off. The one time that Lisa decided to try that, she got in more trouble than she ever had for lying, so she kept fabricating stories.

Fights became more aggressive on both sides. In the midst of an argument, Lisa told her mother that if there were not a penalty for murder, she would have killed her. After that, Lisa's mother constantly threatened to call the police on Lisa if she ever touched or threatened her again. Her mother even found a way to bring her husband's support completely under her control by telling him that he was allowing Lisa to manipulate him against her. He told Lisa not to push him, because if it ever came down to a choice between her and her mother, she would lose.

Lisa began to give up on her family. As they sat in a session with a psychiatrist one afternoon, the doctor asked Lisa if she thought her mother loved her. She responded by saying she did not know. The doctor told her to ask her mother directly, so she did. Her mother responded with a simple "No," and then added that she believed Lisa could change so that she could love her, someday. From that moment on, Lisa knew if she wanted to find acceptance anywhere, it would have to be outside of her home.

In junior high she focused her energies on her schoolwork. It was her escape. She hated home so much that school became a blessing for the time away that it provided. Her grades were excellent. Extracurricular activities were the perfect solution for her and her parents, who wanted her out of the house as much as she wanted to be out of it. She started running cross-country track.

In spite of her newfound success in school and sports, Lisa was sad, lonely, and angry most of the time. There seemed to be nothing that met her need for love and acceptance. Although she had attended church her whole life, she hated God. Her parents claimed to be devout

Christians, so much so that they had never been able to find a denomination that was good enough for them. They had tried six.

Lisa never found anything in those churches to suggest there was a God who loved her. She believed that, if there even was a God, He was mean and angry and just waiting for her to mess up so that He could zap her with a lightning bolt. She thought He must be as ashamed of her as her parents were. By the time she was fifteen, her parents had stopped taking her to church. They were so embarrassed by her that they made her sit in the car while they took her brother to Sunday services.

Still desperate for someone to care about her, Lisa turned to her friends. Most of them had decent families and she found some of the affirmation that she needed there. It was not enough to fill the void in her life so she tried drinking and smoking. They helped the pain, but not for long.

When she was fifteen years old, Lisa got a job working in a veterinary hospital. A friend of hers told her that there was a way to get high by sniffing one of the tranquilizers that was used for the animals. Lisa tried it and found that she enjoyed the high. It made the misery of her life easier to bear.

Her parents discovered the name of the drug written on a piece of paper in Lisa's room and researched it. When they learned that it was a tranquilizer that would be available in an animal hospital, they called her boss and told him that she was abusing the drug. He was forced to fire her, although he had no proof that she was doing what her parents claimed.

Lisa's parents used the incident as an excuse to send her to juvenile court to meet with an officer there. She vehemently denied using drugs. The officer let her know that her parents were seriously considering turning her over to the custody of the state. They had tried a psychiatric clinic for her when she was in the sixth grade with no results, and their insurance would not pay for another one. He told her that if they went ahead with their plan, Lisa would have no choice but to be in the state's custody until she turned eighteen. She had just turned sixteen so that meant two years in a juvenile detention facility.

Lisa was terrified by that possibility. Her mother presented her with one more option—the chance to come to Mercy Ministries. She had received a brochure about the program at a craft show and thought it might be a possibility for Lisa. It was Lisa's only alternative to being turned over to the state.

Determined to do whatever she had to do to avoid the state's custody and get away from her parents, Lisa filled out the application. She only included the information that she thought would help her get into the program. When she had her telephone interview, she stated emphatically that she wanted to come and no one was making her. She promised that she wanted to change, even though all she truly wanted was to escape.

Lisa refused to show any emotion while her mother was with her on her first day in the program. The staff could see from the beginning that she would be an interesting case. Everything about Lisa was hard, from her facial expression to her attitude. She had never experienced true love, and because of how much she had been hurt, her walls were high. We knew that God could change her but wondered if she would let Him.

On the first Sunday that Lisa was at Mercy Ministries, she responded to an invitation to make Jesus her Lord and Savior. In all honesty, when Lisa looks back at that decision now, she sees that it was made more out of a feeling that it was what she was supposed to do rather than something that she wanted to do. Part of her thought that if she would just do her duty and become a Christian, her life would instantly change and be the way she wanted it to be.

That did not happen and Lisa was disappointed. She made up her mind to play her way through the program, fool the staff into thinking that she was doing great, and go back home to live her life the way she wanted to live it. The problem was that she was constantly confronted with people and issues that made it obvious that she was not doing fine.

Living in a home with twenty-five other girls often provoked Lisa's anger. Little things set off explosions that Lisa was unable to control. Her consistently negative attitude and statements did not go unnoticed. She also continued with her distrust of authority figures, making it difficult to peaceably co-exist in an environment where an authority was constantly present.

During the first few months, progress was slow for Lisa. However, there were several things that made an impact on her. The most powerful thing she recognized was that even if she made a mistake and had to be disciplined, the discipline was followed with love. No one turned her away in anger or held a grudge against her. Instead, she was taught how to do the right thing. She became very familiar with the verse that is written on the bottom of the disciplinary form the girls have to sign. It reads, "My son (daughter) do not make light of the Lord's discipline, and do not lose heart when He rebukes you, for the Lord disciplines those He loves." (Hebrews 12:7-8.)

Lisa was beginning to get the idea that life did not have to be like it had been and that she could change. Still, her efforts were half-hearted. She had run into so many roadblocks and barriers already that it was too difficult to try once more. She was almost convinced that she would fail and it was barely worth the effort.

A crucial moment of decision arrived one day when she was called into the program director's office for a meeting. She was informed that her parents did not feel she was serious about the program and were considering bringing her home. It was up to her to choose whether or not she was going to change.

Lisa knew she did not want to be as unhappy as she had been her whole life. During her months at Mercy Ministries, she had glimpsed enough of what a life submitted to God could be like to know that it was a thousand times better than anything she had experienced before. She knew she would not be able to find that at home with her parents or in the custody of the state. Immediately she made the decision that she would put her whole heart into the process of change.

The next months were the fastest months of growth that Lisa experienced. She first focused on learning how to control her anger. She was taught that anger itself is not a problem—even Jesus became angry (John 2:13-16). The problem came when she expressed her anger inappropriately. Ephesians 4:26-27 (NIV) says, *In your anger do not sin. Do not let the sun go down while you are still angry, and do not give the devil a foothold.* It is not the emotion of anger itself that is sin, but when we hold a grudge or give in to an outburst that hurts another, we give Satan a place in our lives.

Lisa began to look beyond her anger to the thoughts and feelings that triggered her emotional response. She realized that it was not another person's actions that made her angry, but the way she thought or felt about them that produced a reaction. For example, if another resident in the program criticized her performance on a work detail, Lisa used to fly into a rage, say hurtful things she did not mean, and storm out of the room. Although she sometimes still reacted negatively, she was able to analyze her response and see that it was not necessarily the comment that hurt her. It was the unspoken message that what she had done was not good enough. That message reminded her of how she had always felt with her mother. That pain was what prompted the outburst.

She learned how to handle the pain so that it no longer controlled her. In the months she had been in the program, she had seen unconditional love in action around her. It was softening her heart towards God. She realized that God was not out to get her for her mistakes. He loved her and did not hold a grudge against her. He also wanted to heal her.

Little by little, Lisa was able to release the hurtful memories to God and allow Him to remove the pain. Just as David did in Psalm 142:2, she poured out her complaint before the Lord, telling Him of all the rejection and lack of acceptance she had experienced while growing up. Again and again God gently reminded her that He was with her and had been with her all along. Psalm 27:10, in the Amplified version, says,

Although my father and mother have forsaken me, yet the Lord will take me up [adopt me as His child]. This became her favorite verse. She clung to it and it helped her through moments of loneliness and despair.

As the pain was relieved, the bitterness that Lisa held in her heart began to disappear as well. She started to see that people were not out to hurt her. At the beginning of her stay, Lisa had been very quick with her sharp tongue, cutting people down with words and hurting them long before they had the chance to hurt her. The more she learned to trust God to protect her, the more she opened up to the staff who offered love and guidance, and to other girls in the program who offered friendship.

Living in the home helped Lisa to mature into the young woman God had called her to be. When she realized that she was not the only person who had problems, her selfishness decreased considerably. She became more sensitive to the needs of others. Learning patience was a key factor in her process of growing up.

At the same time, life in the home allowed her to be a kid for the first time. She had never felt comfortable with her parents, and therefore had never really had fun. While she was in the program, she learned to play. She remembers taking a sheet of plastic and wetting it down with a water hose to make a slip-n-slide in the backyard on a hot summer day. She went to her first baseball games and concerts that year. We also gave her the first birthday party she had had since turning three years old.

That Christmas was the first that was enjoyable for Lisa. Whereas at home she had been left out and made to feel unwanted, here she was right in the middle of everything. She was overwhelmed by the generosity that was shown to her and the other girls in the program. I remember listening to her share what that Christmas meant to her, and how touched I was at the thankfulness and gratitude that poured from her heart.

Unfortunately, in spite of all the changes that were happening in Lisa's life, her relationship with her parents showed no improvement. They refused to believe that Lisa had changed, insisting that she was still lying and manipulating to get her way. Weekend phone calls to her parents became nothing more than chances for them to criticize her and remind her of past mistakes.

Eventually Lisa realized that talking with them set back her progress. It seemed that every time she was able to deal with a wound from the past, they reopened it. She chose to take a break in communicating with them and give herself time to focus on what God was doing in her life.

That infuriated her parents and they threatened to come to the home and pull her out of the program. Lisa handled the situation with a maturity that was surprising for a seventeen-year-old. Although their reactions upset her, she allowed God to deal with her emotions. She stood by what she felt God had told her to do and did not waver in her decision.

Lisa also started to understand that it was going to be impossible for her to return home. Her parents were adamant about not believing that she had changed and they did not want her to return home. They told Lisa's counselor that if she graduated from Mercy Ministries, they would place her in a halfway house until she turned eighteen, or she would have to live on her own. Lisa felt that she would not be able to achieve the dreams and goals that God had placed in her heart as long as her parents continued to control her life. She decided to take their suggestion and pursue legal emancipation.

Lisa also started preparing for the rest of her life. Her heart's desire was to attend a four-year college and study art. She studied for her GED and passed it with flying colors. She also took the SAT exam and scored well above average. Then she began applying to schools and was accepted into her first choice.

With legal emancipation in progress, finances became an issue for Lisa. She applied for financial aid as an independent student, a status not easily granted by most universities. Legal emancipation did not qualify her. She had to meet with the financial aid officers at her school and have letters written on her behalf before the head of the financial aid department made a decision.

At her first meeting with a financial aid counselor, Lisa was told that the school rarely, if ever, granted independent status. The counselor helped her figure out how much money she would need to cover all of her expenses. Lisa's eyes widened at the numbers. She left discouraged but forced herself to remember that there was no circumstance too big for God to handle. He had already rescued her life from misery, and she chose to trust that He would continue to bless her.

The very next day, the counselor called to tell her that she had been granted independent status and that enough aid was available to cover all of her expenses for the first semester! All of the staff and girls rejoiced with Lisa at God's amazing provision for her. After fourteen months, she would finally be able to graduate from the program and go directly to college to begin pursuing her dreams.

During Lisa's graduation ceremony, God prompted me to share Psalm 68:6 (AMP) with her. It states, ***God places the solitary in families.*** I told her that I believed God had placed her in the family of Mercy Ministries, and I committed that we would fulfill that role in her life. I asked her to contact us regularly to keep us updated on her academic progress and told her if she ever needed a place to go for breaks or a weekend away from campus she could call us. We would be her family.

Lisa recently started her third year at college and is doing well. In the beginning, it was tough for her to come out of what she describes as a "God-bubble" at Mercy Ministries and be immersed in the real world. In an environment where she was taught and fed the Word of God on a consistent basis, it became easy to trust God. Then, suddenly, she was on her own with Him and had to put into practice everything she had learned while in the program.

College life has had its ups and downs, but through them all God has proven Himself faithful to her. Even during the times when she doubted His ability to provide He would remind her, "Don't go there, Lisa, because you know me better than that." Her relationship with Him has been tested and "put through the fire," as she says, and it has come out stronger each time.

God continues to amaze her with His provision. Not long ago, a local used car dealership donated a car to Mercy Ministries for the specific purpose of giving it to a graduate. As I prayed about who should receive it, God placed Lisa's name in my heart and in the hearts of several other staff whom I consulted about the decision. When I presented Lisa with the keys, she could hardly speak. She recently told me that she still cries sometimes as she drives around, completely overwhelmed by the goodness of God and the blessings He has placed in her life.

Lisa's relationship with her parents remains strained and that saddens Lisa. She misses them and attempts to communicate with them through e-mail, but they do not respond to her messages. Although it hurts her, she is able to forgive them and let God deal with the pain so that she can move on and continue to walk in His best for her life. Now that she finally believes that she deserves His best, she has set her mind to achieving it and is not willing to let anything stop her.

CHAPTER 11

SHERRY

"Mama," Sherry said casually, "I won't be home until later. My friend and I are going to a party on campus tonight."

"Where is the party?" she asked.

"At one of the fraternity houses where a couple of my friends live. It's no big deal. We won't be late."

"Okay, Sherry. Just be careful."

Sherry smiled at her mother and got ready to leave. Before she could get out the door though, her stepfather caught her gently by the elbow and steered her into the living room.

"Sit down," he said quietly.

Sherry obeyed him and waited.

"Now, your mama may not know what a frat party is, but I do," he said. "I don't want my daughter getting a reputation. You can't set a double standard for those girls at Mercy Ministries while you're working there."

"Oh, Daddy, please," Sherry replied, slightly exasperated. "I'm not doing anything wrong. You know you can trust me."

"You just think about what you're doing and the example you're setting for those girls. How would you feel if one of them saw you at that party tonight?"

Sherry went to the frat party, but she was miserable the whole night. She could not stop thinking about the words her stepfather had spoken. Even though she had been rebelling against her parents for some time now, she still respected him and his opinion greatly. He had always considered her his daughter rather than a stepdaughter, and she thought of him as her father.

His words ran through her mind every time she made a decision that she knew would not be a good example for the girls who were living in the Mercy Ministries home where she was working. She felt the conviction of the Holy Spirit working in her life and it made her extremely uncomfortable.

Still, it was not enough to force her to make new choices. What brought her to that point was something that she never expected.

By her own description, Sherry had been a "good girl" most of her life. She was raised in a Christian home and was active in her church youth group. Most of the time she did what her mother and stepfather told her to do. In truth, however, Sherry was just playing the game. Her heart was not in it.

At seventeen years old, Sherry went through a rebellious stage where she decided that she knew everything. She was tired of being the good girl and tired of the hypocrisy she saw at church. People who sang in the choir on Sunday morning were out in the bars that night, living the lives of people who honor God with their lips but keep their hearts far from Him (Isaiah 29:13). She became very disillusioned and decided that it was time to do things her own way.

In spite of her decision, there was an image that Sherry felt compelled to uphold. For the sake of her family, she continued going to church, acting the part on the outside. Her life was a representation of 2 Timothy 3:5 (NIV), *having a form of godliness but denying its power.*

Sherry soon became a college student with a desire to attend medical school, and she had to work to pay for her education. I was attending the same church as Sherry and her family when she approached me about working in the office of Mercy Ministries. Although she was at a place in her personal life where she was making choices that went against many of the things she knew were right, Sherry still had a sincere desire to help. In spite of her age, I hired her part-time as a runner in the office.

It was during this time that Sherry's stepfather sat her down in their living room to talk about the example she was setting for the girls.

From that point on, she began to feel conviction about her lifestyle. Jesus told his disciples in John 16:8-11 that one of the functions of the Holy Spirit is to convict the world of sin. Often, what we refer to as our conscience helping us determine what is right and wrong is actually the work of the Holy Spirit inside our hearts. We have the ability to choose whether or not we will listen to that still, small voice and bring our flesh under the control of the Holy Spirit. First Timothy 4:2 warns that our conscience can become seared, meaning that if we ignore the prompting of the Holy Spirit long enough, we will reach a point where we enter into sin without any sense of wrongdoing. This leaves us in a dangerous position where Satan can set us up for destruction as a result of our own choices.

Sherry continued to override her conscience and make choices that she knew were not in her best interest, including in the area of dating. She and the youth pastor's son began a serious relationship when Sherry was eighteen. Michael and Sherry had been friends for a long time. Their families were good friends, and from the time they were about fourteen, Sherry and her date and Michael and his date would go out together. Michael taught Sherry how to drive. They were just typical kids.

Sherry realizes now that much of what she was looking for in her relationship with Michael was the love and acceptance she had never received from her biological father. Her mother had become pregnant with Sherry's older brother at the age of fourteen and married the birthfather. Then, Sherry was born when her mother was sixteen. When Sherry was seven years old, her father left her mother for another woman.

Sherry's mother remarried when Sherry was ten years old. Although Sherry and her stepfather always had an excellent relationship—he never called her his stepdaughter, only his daughter—Sherry still suffered rejection issues from the choice her father made to leave his family. She wanted to feel special to somebody.

Those feelings and the peer pressure from her friends, who continually made snide comments to Sherry about her virginity, pushed her towards a decision to become sexually active. On New Year's Eve, Michael and Sherry left a church service and had sex for the first time.

The sense of conviction in Sherry's heart was growing stronger and stronger. Each time she made a decision to sin, she heard her stepfather's voice reminding her about the double standard she was setting for the girls at Mercy Ministries, even though they were not aware of her behavior away from the office.

One afternoon, Sherry was sitting in a house meeting with the girls in which I was addressing some issues of strife that had surfaced in the home. I began with Proverbs 28:13 (NKJV), *He who covers his sins will not prosper, But whoever confesses and forsakes them will have mercy.*

Sherry did not hear anything else that was said in the meeting. She was overwhelmed with conviction and knew that it was time to do something about it. "This is the day," she thought. "I have to tell Nancy what I've been doing. I'll lose my job, but I have to do what is right."

When Sherry came to talk to me, she found me sitting in my office eating a bag of potato chips. Sherry remembers that as she told me about her behavior, including the events that took place on New Year's Eve, I continued to calmly eat my chips. Sherry finished her story and waited, expecting to be fired. She actually wanted to be fired; at least that would have made her feel better.

"Well," I said slowly, "you need to repent."

Sherry nodded and told me that she had done so.

"You can't keep doing that and work here at the same time, you know."

"I know," Sherry replied.

"I just want you to get some help," I said. "I'll set up some counseling sessions for you with the pastor of the church."

Sherry waited for another moment. "That's it?" she finally asked. "I can still work here?"

"Yes, you can still work here," I replied. "Now, if you're pregnant, that's a different story."

Relieved, Sherry assured me that she was not pregnant and left my office. She was amazed by the unconditional love that had been shown to her. That was something she had heard about but had not seen put into action. Christians that she had been exposed to were more often critical and judgmental, caught up in religion like the Pharisees of Jesus' days who followed the rules but missed out on the relationship God offered them. These are the people to whom Jesus was talking when He rebuked them for cleaning the outside of the cup but letting the inside remain full of greed and self-indulgence (Matthew 23:25).

Two weeks later, Sherry found out that she was pregnant. Although she was devastated, she found it was easy to confess to me this time because she had already told me about the poor decisions she had made. Sherry told me about the pregnancy before she even told her parents.

"First of all, you have to tell your parents," I informed her. Then I thought for a moment. "You know, I take in girls from all across the country that I've never seen before, so I don't see why I wouldn't take you in if you want to come. You'll have to resign, of course."

Sherry was amazed again. I talked with her about how difficult it would be to go through the pain and embarrassment of telling the girls about her mistakes and going from being an authority figure to a peer. It would be an extremely humbling experience for her, and I wanted to be sure that she was ready to handle that. She believed she was. Sherry went home and told her parents about the pregnancy. Together they decided that the best option was for her to go to Mercy Ministries. A few weeks later, she moved in.

Sherry's church did not react favorably to the situation. I had initially intended to set up counseling for her with the pastor, but the leadership there was adamant that Sherry should leave town. I could understand the difficult position the church was in with both birthparents in the congregation, but I was also in a rather sticky situation. This was a young woman whom I had hired to work part-time in a ministry to unwed mothers, and now she was unmarried and pregnant.

The temptation was certainly to ship her out of town; it would have been the easiest thing. From the beginning, however, God had told me that I was supposed to take in anyone who sincerely wanted help. I did not see how I could help strangers and not one of my own. God reminded me of the verse in Galatians 6:1 which says that we who are "spiritual" should "gently restore" one who is caught in a sin. Sherry needed love, not condemnation. She needed mercy, not judgment. The church leaders called me into meetings and challenged my decision, but I was sure that I was doing what God wanted me to do and I stood firm. Sherry's family left that church as a result of the confrontation.

It was an awkward transition for Sherry to become a girl in the program after working in the office for some time. We held a house meeting to discuss the unique details of Sherry's situation with the girls. I explained that Sherry needed help and that she was going to be coming to Mercy Ministries.

The room was very quiet as I spoke, and Sherry told me later that she felt like she could have died. She sat there and cried, devastated by the way she had let down those girls she cared so much about. There was silence for a moment when I finished. Finally, one girl spoke up.

"Can she have the empty bed in my room?" she asked.

A huge sigh of relief escaped Sherry. All of the girls reached out to her, accepted her, and did not judge her. They were glad that she was there, and that helped Sherry to be glad that she was there as well. She moved in and devoted herself to working the program.

From the beginning, Sherry planned to keep her baby. Her family and Michael's family wanted them to get married. They tried joint counseling, but it was not successful. Then Sherry discovered that Michael had also gotten another girl pregnant, and she realized that he would never be faithful to her. She refused to marry him. Michael married the other girl instead.

It was late in her pregnancy when Sherry finally realized that as much as she wanted to parent her child, she could not. Her parents had six children of their own, and three of them were kindergarten age and younger. Although they said they would adopt the baby and raise it as their own, Sherry did not think she could do that. She felt it would be shifting the responsibility to her parents, and she had been raised to face the consequences of her own decisions. Sherry did not think she could stand watching her child be raised by someone else within her own family.

Her parents made it clear that they would be supportive of Sherry, no matter what she chose to do. Sherry struggled with her decision, desperately wanting to parent but feeling as though she could not. At one point, her counselor sat down with her and taught her how to balance a checkbook and manage her money. She helped Sherry understand all the costs of raising a child, from diapers and formula to doctor's bills and car seats, cribs, and strollers. Our philosophy at Mercy Ministries is to give the pregnant girls a solid reality check about both parenting and placing for adoption so that they can have all the information they need to make a good decision. Part of that process includes an in-depth look at finances.

It was then that Sherry realized that she simply could not keep her baby. In addition to her lack of financial stability, Sherry knew she was not emotionally or mentally ready to raise a child. She was adamant about finishing college and knew that raising a baby at the same time would be extremely difficult. She also felt strongly that a child needs both a mom and a dad in the home.

On top of that, Michael's new wife was pregnant at the same time and rumors were already flying. Sherry did not want her child to have a half-brother or sister in the same town. She wanted the baby away from all of that.

Sherry decided that she was going to choose adoption for her child, in spite of her fear that the price she would pay would be her sanity. Her mind made up, she went to her counselor and told her what her decision was, expecting to hear an "okay." Instead, her counselor told her that she had to make sure that it was God.

Sherry was instructed to continue praying about it and expect God to confirm to her if adoption was the right decision for her. He instructs us in Proverbs 3:5-6 (NKJV) to *Trust in the Lord with all your heart, and lean not on your own understanding; In all your ways acknowledge Him and He shall direct your paths.* Sherry wanted a quick confirmation from her counselor that she was doing the right thing, but we wanted Sherry to be firmly convinced in her heart that her choice was what God had instructed her to do.

Sometimes the girls want the staff to make the decision for them, so that they can either be released from the responsibility or so that they can shift the responsibility for the consequences of their choices to someone else. I have trained my staff to refuse to do that. Over the years, I have seen many girls come through Mercy Ministries and make decisions that appear to be the opposite of what circumstances would dictate. Yet, they have turned out to be the right choice because it was God's plan, not man's. I do not want to be the one who stands in the way of what God wants to do! I always try to remember Proverbs 16:25 (NIV) in such situations: *There is a way that seems right to a man, but in the end it leads to death.* That is why we always make sure the girls have the freedom to make their decision on their own, between themselves and God.

Sherry sought the Lord on her own, and He was faithful to His promise found in Jeremiah 29:13 (NIV), *You will seek me and find me when you seek me with all your heart.* Once Sherry was sure that it was the right decision, she asked me to find an adoptive couple for her. She did not give me many specifics at all. Her one stated desire was that the couple not be in full-time ministry, but that they be "normal working people." Sherry had unfortunately been exposed to such hypocrisy in church leadership that she did not want her child to grow up in a similar family.

Sherry prayed every day for a family that valued education. She never expressed her desire to me or to the staff, but Sherry truly wanted her child to have the opportunity to go to college one day. Since education was so important to her, she asked God to provide a family that shared her opinions.

A few weeks later, when Sherry was less than a month away from her due date, I returned from a speaking engagement and called Sherry into my office. I had met a couple who were friends with the pastor. Both the staff member who traveled with me on that occasion and I felt that they might be the right couple for Sherry. My traveling companion had placed a baby for adoption through the program some time earlier and had been a strong encouragement to Sherry throughout her struggle to make a decision regarding her child.

This couple had no children. They had tried to adopt through another agency three years previously, only to have the plans fall through when the birthmother changed her mind at the last minute. They were devastated and had not tried again since then. I had told them briefly about Sherry's situation and encouraged them to put an application in with Mercy Ministries to adopt.

Sherry listened to what I had to say and left the meeting with much to ponder. A few days later, she came back to me and asked for more information about the potential adoptive couple. It was then that I told Sherry about their professions. Both parents had college degrees. The husband was a businessman who owned his own company, and the wife was a teacher in a gifted and talented program.

When Sherry heard that, she did not need to look at the profiles of any other couples. She knew she had found the right family for her child. God had given her all the desires of her heart, both spoken and unspoken.

Sherry delivered a healthy baby boy three weeks early. When the staff called the family to tell them she was in labor, they heard the whole room erupt in a frenzy on the other end of the line. The call had coincided with a baby shower that the couple's family and friends had organized to help them get ready for instant parenthood!

Each girl who chooses adoption through Mercy Ministries is able to make her own decisions regarding the amount of contact she can have with the adoptive family, as long as the family is in agreement. Sherry opted for a relatively closed adoption, choosing not to meet the family and to communicate only through letters and pictures. She did, however, request that her counselor be the one to present the baby to the adoptive couple. The placement was done on the couple's fifteenth wedding anniversary. This was not planned on our part, but it was obvious that God's timing was involved on that very special day.

Sherry cried a lot, alone, after placing the baby. It never meant that she had changed her mind. She was simply hurting over the difficult choice that she had made, even though she knew beyond a shadow of a doubt that it was the right one. Taking the right road is not always easy. In fact, it is rarely the easy choice. Jesus warned His followers in Matthew 7:14 that the road that leads to life is narrow and often the hardest path to take. The rewards, however, are well worth the price!

Sherry made it through those times of grief by thinking about all the good things that had happened as a result of placing her baby. She knew how much his new family wanted him and trusted that he would be fine. She heard about all the joy he was bringing to his parents and grandparents. The adoptive father's brother had died a few years earlier and the couple chose to name the baby after him. That brought much needed healing to the still grieving mother, as well as to the rest of the family.

Sherry graduated from the program shortly after giving birth, grateful for all of the opportunities that Mercy Ministries had given her. She says now that the "program is not for wimps" because of the difficult process that each girl must undergo while there. It is a process of change. As the girls are taught the Word every day and they make the decision to order their lives accordingly, they cannot help but change. They also receive biblically based counseling that reinforces the principles of God's Word taught through the various classes offered as a part of the program.

Sherry was diligent in her effort to work the program, doing all that was expected of her and sometimes more. At some point, Sherry knew that she had to internalize the things that were being taught. James 1:22 tells us that we must be doers of the Word, not just hearers. Sherry had spent her life playing the game of Christianity and that had only gotten her in trouble. Mercy Ministries was not a place where she could "ride the pine" of a church pew any longer, hearing the Word but not being changed by it.

She was confronted with tough love and realized that she would have to make her decisions based on what God wanted her to do, rather than on the opinions of her parents or someone else in the church. She had to choose for herself. Sherry made that choice and committed herself fully to God and His plan for her life rather than her own.

Not long after graduating from the program Sherry married a wonderful young Christian man she had met previously through her brother. She also went to a four-year nursing school and finished her degree. In her heart she felt that she needed to give back. Sherry decided to volunteer time at Mercy Ministries, offering to do whatever was needed, from running errands to teaching class to scrubbing toilets. Sherry began coming to the home to do both formal and informal childbirth preparation classes with the girls.

The staff at Mercy Ministries had been praying for months for favor with the delivery room nurses at the hospital the girls went to, and at about this same time, Sherry was offered a position there as one of the delivery room nurses. She became a friendly face for the girls to see when the time came for them to deliver their babies. It was another example of a divine appointment that only God could have orchestrated.

The first time a Mercy Ministries girl delivered a baby after Sherry accepted the position, the girl had labored all night before Sherry came on duty. When Sherry arrived, she discovered that the girl had let everyone on the shift know about Sherry's story, not knowing that she had not chosen to share that information herself.

It was difficult for Sherry, now that everyone knew about her situation. Until then she had really wanted to move on and forget about her past. She realized, however, that even though it would be easier not to deal with it, it would be wrong. She knew that she could not be helped the way that she had been and not help someone else in return.

Although it can be draining to go through the emotions time and again, God always refills her. Sherry knows it was God-ordained for her to work there. She can cry with the girls as they work through their emotions, knowing their pain. It helps them to know that someone else understands. It also helps them to know that she can truly understand the joy that will allow them to get through the pain.

The other nurses began calling Sherry when one of "her girls" came in to deliver so that Sherry could attend to them. Because of Sherry's love for them, and because of the difference that the nurses could see in the girls from Mercy Ministries, the other nurses also began taking special care of "Sherry's girls."

As Sherry continued to volunteer at the home, God brought her more opportunities to minister to the girls the way she had received ministry. One afternoon, when she stopped by, the staff asked her to talk with a young woman who was very close to delivery and still extremely uncertain about what she wanted to do with her baby. Remembering the influence that one staff member with a similar experience had had on her, Sherry agreed to talk to the young woman.

She told the girl all about her story, how God had picked the perfect couple for her and how Sherry had known it without a doubt. She told her about the grief process that she would go through and how she would go back and forth through the stages before she finally reached her healing. Some days she would cry and other days she would be okay, but overall she would know that she made the right decision. The joy would be worth the pain.

Sherry left that conversation wondering if she had said the right things to the girl, and whether her story had made any difference in her life. A few months later she received a phone call from the young woman. She had delivered a healthy baby boy and placed him with a couple who had already adopted a son through Mercy Ministries. Sherry began to shake. She knew, as soon as the girl told her about the other child the couple had adopted, that this girl's baby had been placed in the same family with Sherry's son. Sherry now felt like she had a hand in the couple adopting both of their children and was overwhelmed with emotion.

There was a time following that second placement when this young woman was still unsure about her decision. I decided to let her know that the couple she had chosen was the same couple who adopted Sherry's baby. Because of her conversation with Sherry, this girl knew immediately that she had done the right thing. From that moment on, she had perfect peace.

Today, Sherry has her master's degree as a women's health nurse practitioner. She takes care of pregnant women every day. God used her experience to make her strong so that she can minister to others. She recognizes how many times she has been strategically placed in the delivery room so that she can help bring others the healing that she once received. Her life is a now a living example of 2 Corinthians 1:4 (NIV), which explains that God *comforts us in all our troubles, so that we can comfort those in any trouble with the comfort we ourselves have received from God.*

The girls always come and see her after their regular doctors appointments, and Sherry gives them an ultrasound. She is still often in the delivery room when the Mercy Ministries girls have their babies. She also has opportunities to reach out to women and girls who are not associated with the ministry but are hurting in the same ways. Time and again Sherry has seen how her story and unique ability to relate to their pain has broken down walls of bitterness and pain.

After placing her first son for adoption, Sherry thought she would never have another child. She did not think that she had any maternal instinct because she had to work so hard to suppress it in order to avoid the pain and grief and numbness that came from giving her baby away. However, she and her husband now have a five-year-old son who is the joy of both of their lives.

She remembers the moment that she found out she was pregnant. It occurred to her in the middle of a class during nursing school that she had not had a period in a while. She went to the doctor and he confirmed her pregnancy. Instantly Sherry was overwhelmed with excitement and fell to her knees to thank God. Sherry somehow knew that because she had given up the most precious gift possible, her first son, that God was now giving back to her. She was elated!

Sherry loves being a mother and that is even further confirmation to her that she made the right decision. Her first son is healthy and happy, living in a home with a younger brother. They both receive all the love and care that they deserve. Sherry has been able to complete her education and now has the family she always desired. Each day she is able to count her blessings and thank God for the way He has worked in her life. She is overwhelmed by His grace and mercy and, most of all, by His love.

To this day, Sherry continues giving her love and time to those who walk through the doors of Mercy Ministries feeling alone and afraid. She remembers what it was like. As she reaches out as a special friend sent by God, Sherry is one of God's precious instruments used to take away the fear.

CHAPTER 12

AMY

"Ladies and gentlemen, contemporary Christian artists Point of Grace!"
Amy sat, arms folded across her chest, trying her best to look bored. She was enjoying the concert, but she did not want anyone to know. As far as her friends knew, she was against all of this Christian stuff, although she attended a Christian college and lived with a pastor's family. It was much safer for Amy if they continued to think of her as a heathen.

Halfway through the concert, the lights went down in the auditorium and a video started to play. Faces of different girls flashed on the screen, talking about things that Amy knew way too much about already—abuse, anger, rape, suicide attempts. Then they started talking about having been healed and set free from all of it through a place called Mercy Ministries of America.

Anger began to burn inside Amy. "That would be great," she thought, "if it could really happen." There was no way someone could be healed from all the things that she had been through. A part of her wanted it to be true, but she could not believe it was real. She grew furious that Mercy Ministries would put out such obviously false information.

During the intermission, she walked out to the Mercy Ministries table. She heard someone say that books were free with a donation, so she handed the girl a ten-dollar bill. Amy was given a book and a brochure but she slid the brochure back on the table. She did not want to appear too interested.

Alone in her bedroom, Amy did not have to pretend. She sat down with the book and read it faster than she had ever read anything before. Every story amazed her. Each sounded like real life, but the ending was never right. All of the people ended up healed and happy and loving God, and that was not possible for anyone who had been through such things. She was proof of that.

The anger welled up inside her and she fired off a letter to Mercy Ministries. She told them that the book was a bunch of crap. None of it was real—there was no such thing as unconditional love. Anyone who had ever gotten to know her had stopped loving her. God would never break through to her. She would not let Him.

A few days later, there was a message on the answering machine from someone at Mercy Ministries calling to check on her. Amy was stunned. She did not remember writing her phone number on the letter. She certainly had not expected to hear from anyone after trashing the program and everything that they believed.

When no one was around to overhear her, Amy called back. She was unsure how it happened, but by the end of the conversation she had agreed to let them send her an application. There was no harm in it. She might as well fill it out and tell them what she really thought. She had a foolproof plan ready for ending her life and nothing was going to stop her this time. If this was her chance to prove God a liar, she would jump at the opportunity.

Amy had spent most of her life acting tough, trying to convince everybody that she did not care. For the most part, she had succeeded. Her hard shell only masked an unbelievable amount of pain that tortured her on a regular basis. Amy was trapped in a very dark place with little hope for escape.

As a young girl, Amy had been a tenderhearted and loving child. She loved her mother and her older sister very much, but she was a daddy's girl. She loved to hunt and fish with her father more than anything. He took her with him on all of his trips. A friend of her father's, Mike, also went with them. They spent hours together in the woods, on the lake, or just sitting on the tailgate of the truck and talking.

One evening, when Amy was seven years old, she was sitting between them on the tailgate when Mike put his hand on her leg. She did not pay much attention until he moved his hand and started touching her in places that she did not think he should be touching her. Amy was sure he did not realize what he was doing. After all, her dad was right there with them, even though it was too dark for him to see what was happening.

She moved away from Mike, scooting closer to her dad. When Mike did not stop, she jumped down from the tailgate. Later that evening, when her dad could not hear, Mike told Amy that if she ever wanted him to do that again, she should let him know.

"Do what?" Amy responded, pretending to not know what he was talking about, and then ran off before he could answer. She knew then that he knew exactly what he was doing. She wanted to get as far away from him as she could.

There was no way to stay away from Mike, however, unless she stopped spending time with her father. Amy was too embarrassed to tell him what had happened. Besides, Mike was his best friend, and she did not want to hurt her father in any way. She kept it to herself and tried to avoid Mike.

That was impossible. He always found a way to get her alone when they were on a trip together. It did not matter that her father was there, or even if Amy's whole family was with them. She would threaten to scream, but she knew he had planned it so that no one would be close enough to hear. Amy was afraid he might hurt her family if she told them what was happening to her.

She learned to go somewhere else in her mind and think other thoughts while he abused her. Then he started telling her that she must be enjoying it because she never stopped it. Amy believed him, and she lived with overwhelming guilt and shame. She never told anyone. Mike's abuse went on for nine years.

When Amy was eight years old, a cousin also began to sexually abuse her. He was five years older than she was and he took advantage of her. Whenever he could, he included his friends. Amy could not tell anyone what he was doing; it would destroy the family. There was already a great deal of tension between her mother and his. She knew his mother would blame her if she told anyone about the abuse.

That aunt and cousin were very active in the church Amy's father had grown up in and where the family still attended. Amy heard her mother talk about what a strong Christian boy her cousin was, and she heard her aunt brag about her own holiness. It did not take long for Amy to decide that she wanted nothing to do with God or His people. She attended church only because her parents made her go.

As the abuse continued, Amy became numb to life. She thought the only reason for her existence was to be a man's plaything. She withdrew further and further into herself, choosing to spend most of her time alone. No one seemed to notice that anything was wrong, even though she was sure it was written all over her face.

Anger began to take root in Amy. Even though she knew her father had no idea what Mike was doing to her, she felt set up by him every time he left her alone on one of their trips. Deep inside, she felt that he should have known how his trusted friend was tormenting his daughter.

Her mother was too involved in other things to notice Amy's pain. She was hurt that Amy preferred to be with her father, so she started spending more time with Amy's sister who enjoyed staying at home and learning to cook and sew. Her mother also started babysitting other children and they demanded a lot of her time.

As Amy watched her mom hold other little girls, she grew jealous. When she competed for her mother's attention, she was pushed away and told that "Mama has a new baby." Her parents laughed at her when she became angry. She started taking it out on the other children by being mean, sometimes physically hurting them. Amy's parents punished her but never realized that her intense anger might be coming from anything other than jealousy.

By the age of nine, Amy had come to the point where she did not want anything from anybody. She could not get the kind of love she craved from her family, and the attention she was getting from Mike and her cousin was exactly what she did not want. She started pushing everyone away from her, trying the only way she knew to protect herself from being hurt even more.

The only thing that offered Amy any kind of enjoyment was being involved in sports. It seemed someone always found something wrong in everything else she did. So she stopped trying to do anything else and focused solely on sports. Her father had taught her to play all kinds of ball and she was an excellent athlete. Softball, basketball, and volleyball became the only things that made her life worth living.

By the age of thirteen, Amy had successfully pushed her family away. Her parents thought she was disrespectful and rebellious and they blamed her for all the family problems. Her sister would not even acknowledge her at school. Amy was frustrated and angry. There seemed to be no end of the pain in sight. Mike's abuse continued. He had progressed from molesting her to raping her on a regular basis. She decided everyone would be better off if she was no longer around.

She wrote a suicide letter and addressed it to her best friend. Jana was the youth pastor's daughter and one year older than Amy. Despite her negative attitude towards God, Amy had become close to Jana and her family. She saw in them what she was missing in her own family—stability, caring, and openness. She could talk to Jana's mother, even though she never chose to open up about anything too personal. They were the only people who seemed to truly care about her. Although she was not willing to admit it, Amy wanted the relationship with God that she saw in them.

Amy's life was so painful that she wanted to die. She planned to overdose on over-the-counter medications, but wanted to wait until after her last volleyball game. She hid the note inside her purse and left it in her bedroom.

Her mother found the note while Amy was at the volleyball game and confronted her about it. Amy was furious that her mother had gone through her things. Her mother was furious that the note placed most of the blame on her. Finally, Amy said she had been angry when she wrote the note and that she did not mean what she had written. Her mother told her to rip up the note in front of her and it would be over.

Amy ripped up the note but it was far from over. The rift between her and her mother grew wider every day. The further apart they drifted, the closer Amy became with Jana's mother. She was there with the love that Amy had always wanted from her own mother. There was so much anger built up, that Amy turned her mother away even when she was offered love.

An obsession with suicide and death began to consume Amy. She wanted to learn all about it. She read everything she could find, including the obituaries in the newspaper. Every time she was assigned a research project for school, she reported on suicide. People told her that she was morbid, but no one took the time to find out if there was something behind her obsession.

Jana's mother recognized there was a serious problem. She did everything she could to change Amy's mind. Her love and attention were probably the only things that kept Amy alive during that time. She told Amy, "If for no other reason, don't kill yourself because of me. I would be devastated." Amy could not understand why her life would matter that much to anyone.

Amy overdosed a number of times but never took enough pills to seriously hurt herself. She would cut herself, but not deep enough for anyone to notice. As much as she wanted to die, she was more afraid that a serious attempt would fail. She was afraid of ending up in the hospital and having to answer questions.

Amy did not want anybody to try to figure her out. She just wanted somebody to love her. The problem was that whenever anyone tried to love her, they couldn't get through the many walls she had built. The one thing she wanted most was what she continually pushed away.

Amy was convinced that God did not and could not love her. She had grown up hearing that God was in control and that He protects those He loves. She thought He must not love her because He had never protected her. No one had. She blamed Him for everything. Before long, she hated Him.

It seemed that Amy hated everyone. She had a reputation for being mean and people generally stayed away from her. In sports, she knocked down anyone who was in her way and went after anyone who knocked her down. Kids at school would say, "There are two people in this school you don't want to mess with, and Amy's one of them." Amy liked it that way. As long as people were afraid of her, they stayed out of her business.

When Amy was not thinking about death or attempting suicide, she was dreaming of ways to get away from her parents. She boldly told her mother that she would leave as soon as she turned eighteen. Her mother reacted defensively, telling her she would never make it on her own. Amy was determined to prove her wrong.

The only way of escape she could see, other than suicide, was to go to college. During her junior and senior year of high school, Amy pulled herself together just enough to get straight A's. She desperately wanted to get a scholarship so that she would not be dependent on her parents for anything.

During the middle of the night on her eighteenth birthday, Amy moved out of her house and in with Jana and her family. Amy's parents were extremely upset because they all went to the same church. Her mother had worked hard to portray the image of a perfect family. She assumed people would talk and their family would look bad. She told everyone in town that it was all Amy's fault. She was the "wild child," an angry and rebellious teenager who was out of control.

Amy's mother called family members and told them that Amy had ruined the family. They called Amy and berated her for what she was doing to her mother. No matter how much their words hurt, Amy kept the pain hidden beneath a layer of anger. She pretended she did not care what anyone thought. "Yeah, I ruined the family," she would respond. "So what?"

Amy did receive a scholarship and she enrolled at a Christian college. She wanted nothing to do with God but the school that offered the scholarship was the one Jana attended. It was also the same denomination in which Jana's father was a pastor, and it pleased him that she was planning to attend. She decided she could handle all the talk about God as long as it kept everyone off her case.

Amy roomed with Jana during her first year, but Jana had already been there for a year and the friendship had become distant during the time they had spent apart. Jana had her own friends, and she and Amy went their separate ways. Amy found her own group of friends, but they were the wrong kind.

One of Amy's new friends was heavily into witchcraft. Amy was more than willing to learn about casting spells and reading palms. She had always been fascinated by the spirit world. From the time she was four years old, she had watched horror movies with her family. When her eight-year-old sister was too scared to sleep, it was Amy who comforted her.

Nothing scared Amy. She had learned to assume the role of the killer rather than the victim while she watched the movies. That way, she was not scared of who was coming around the corner. In her mind, it was her coming around the corner. For so much of her life, she had been the victim. This was her one chance to experience the other side, even if it was just for a short time.

During her freshman year, Amy began dating David, a strong Christian boy on campus. Even though she was not interested in a relationship with God for herself, Amy figured if she married a guy who was a believer, he would not be mean to her. She truly loved David and he loved her. They dated for the entire year until he went away for the summer on a missions trip.

When he returned, Amy could not wait to see him. She was blindsided by his response. He told her that while he was away, God had told him to break up with her. Amy was completely stunned, hurt, and angry. David's rejection was one more reason for her to hate God and to believe that He hated her.

Immediately Amy turned to her old friend—suicide. She drove to the edge of town and parked her car on the train tracks. Normally a train came through every thirty minutes. She had hidden the car so well that there would not be enough time for the train to stop. She watched the clock as she waited to die. Thirty minutes went by, and then an hour. After an hour and a half, she was so frustrated that she threw the car into gear and drove away.

Barely five minutes later, as Amy sat at a red light, she heard the train come through town. Infuriated, she began screaming and cursing at God. "Why won't You let me die? I hate You! I trash Your name in front of everyone whenever I have the chance! Why won't You just let me die?"

Amy knows now that even as she was saying those things, God understood. The Bible says in 1 Samuel 16:7 (NIV), **Man looks at the outward appearance, but the Lord looks at the heart.** Even though Amy wanted people to think that she hated God, He knew the truth. She was hurting and did not know any other way to deal with her pain. After that experience, Amy remained very suicidal but did not make any serious attempts for a time. As much as she hated to admit it, she knew God had prevented her last one, and she was convinced that another one would not work.

While not actively pursuing death, Amy let her life fall apart. Depression began to rule her. She slept through all of her classes. She got up only to go to work, go out late at night with friends, or to sit down in the lounge and watch television.

Vanessa and Deborah lived in Amy's dorm. They began to learn her pattern. They had heard the stories about her, about how mean she was and how she would leave nasty messages on people's doors. Still, they could see that she was hurting and needed God. They decided to become her friends and started timing their trips through the lounge to coincide with when they knew she would be there.

They said hello each night as they walked by. When they tried to have a conversation with her, Amy growled at them, but it did not turn them off. Eventually their persistence prevailed and they became friends. Because they proved to her that they cared, she started leaving the television behind to go to their Bible study. She made it clear that she was just there to sit and listen, and that she did not believe any of that "God stuff."

Amy had not dated anyone since David had hurt her so badly. She met a young man at work and they became friends. Late one night, he asked Amy to meet him and she agreed. Vanessa and Deborah asked her not to go. From what she had told them, the guy seemed like bad news. Amy ignored their advice and went anyway. It turned out to be a decision she would regret.

He forced himself on Amy that night, even though she told him no. All Amy could think about was how much she wanted to die. Vanessa and Deborah were waiting up for her when she got home. They could see she had been crying and guessed what had happened. Amy denied it until they asked her if they could pray for her. The rage inside her exploded.

"God does not protect people!" she screamed. "Yeah, he did rape me. What's it to you? What's your God gonna do about it? He ain't gonna do nothing!" She stormed out of the room and slammed the door behind her.

Frightened by the intensity of her anger, Vanessa and Deborah felt they had to get help for Amy. They took a letter she had written about her depression and suicidal thoughts and showed it to a counselor. They also told her about the rape. The counselor brought Amy in on the pretense of talking to her about another friend of hers who had committed suicide. In the course of the conversation, the counselor pulled out Amy's letter. She asked her if she still wanted to die.

Amy would not answer. She was enraged that Vanessa and Deborah had broken her confidence, and she was determined not to share any more information. The counselor admitted her to a psychiatric hospital for 72 hours because she refused to say that she did not want to die. Amy knew that the hospital cared most about the insurance money they would get from her. If she acted happy, she would get out. She played the game and was released three days later.

The depression continued. She quit her job and spent most of her time sleeping. Eventually she forgave Vanessa and Deborah but stayed only on the fringes of their lives, refusing to become more involved. The walls around her were getting higher and higher.

For her 21st birthday, a friend took Amy to the liquor store and bought her a bottle of vodka. Amy had never drank before and for the next six months she remained drunk. Alcohol made everyone think she was happy and they stopped asking her so many questions. The best part was that when she was drunk, she did not have to feel the pain that was always inside her.

Over Christmas break, Amy traveled with a friend and her boyfriend, Philip, to sing at another friend's wedding. To everyone's surprise, especially her own, Amy and Philip ended up sleeping together that weekend. Neither had intended for it to happen, but it did.

It was the first time that Amy had voluntarily slept with anyone. She had barely let any of her other boyfriends hold her hand, and the only sexual experiences she had had were forced on her against her will. As far as she was concerned, her choice was another failure to add to the list in her life. She had decided that she was not going to have sex before she was married and she had messed that up too.

It became easier for Amy to decide that nothing mattered. She had no desire to live. Philip broke up with his girlfriend and started dating Amy. Everyone on campus blamed her for the breakup. Everyone found out they were sleeping together and blamed her for that too. Philip was a pastor's son and the praise and worship leader at his church. They thought Amy's bad influence was bringing him down. She never told anyone that he had initiated the whole relationship. It was not worth the effort.

For the next semester, Amy remained constantly drunk. She and Philip were together every chance they had. Vanessa and Deborah remained concerned about her. Amy knew they disapproved of her lifestyle, even though they never judged her. Amy knew the choices she was making were wrong When she was around them, she felt convicted so she did her best to avoid them. Her own conscience was speaking to her, just as the Bible describes in Romans 2:15.

Amy decided that she was going to end her life once and for all. She formulated a foolproof plan. She would take a full bottle of pills, drink a bottle of vodka, cut her wrists, and then sit on the train tracks. This time, she wrote nothing down and told no one. Nothing was going to stop her. She would do it at the end of the semester.

That spring, Amy's roommate asked Amy to go with her to a Point of Grace concert. Initially, Amy turned her down. She had been listening to their music only because Vanessa and Deborah sang their songs in a campus group and they let her listen when they practiced. They even gave her a tape. Amy told them it was fine but that she preferred her heavy metal music. Privately, she listened to Point of Grace whenever she was alone.

Amy thought it would be too much of a risk to go to the concert. She knew that if it looked like she was interested in spiritual things, there would instantly be all kinds of pressure on her that she was not prepared to handle. She did not want to admit to herself that her heart was softening, much less let her friends know.

At the last minute, though, someone else offered to go with her. She really wanted to hear Point of Grace, so she decided to go. It was that night that she heard about Mercy Ministries for the first time. Then she wrote her angry letter, which was followed up by the phone call from my assistant. She received the application just a few days before the date she had set for her suicide. When she read it, she felt that it did not force religion on her and she could simply answer the questions.

Amy had nothing to lose, so she filled it out honestly. Her answers were short and to the point, but they spoke volumes about her pain. One of the last questions asked what she wanted God to do in her life while she was at Mercy Ministries. Her answer read, "I don't think God can do anything for me. None of this unconditional love stuff is real. He can't do anything for me."

The staff recognized that Amy's angry and sarcastic answers were a desperate cry for help. She was clearly a young woman with no hope. Her application was prayed over and everyone agreed that she needed to come in right away. We knew that God could help her and we knew she needed it immediately. We did not know that her suicide plan was set for only days away—but God did.

Amy was more than surprised that she was accepted and she decided to come. No one understood her decision. Jana's family took it as a personal offense, thinking that by leaving Amy was saying that they could not help her. Amy knew that they had done everything they could and she tried to explain that to them. She told them that if there was anyone who could help her, it was God.

The truth was that Amy had no expectations that even God would help her. She came in with the attitude that she was going to prove everyone wrong. There was no such thing as unconditional love. God could not love her. No one could. She was too hard, too mean, and too buried within her walls. She came to conquer, not to be conquered. She would prove God wrong, and then she would die.

From the beginning, Amy ran into love all around her. People accepted her just as she was and did not try to force any kind of beliefs on her. They simply cared about her, no matter how she reacted. She hid within her protective walls and watched, waiting for the caring to end.

The adjustment process was difficult for Amy, as it is for many of the young women who come into the program. Unlike others, though, Amy did not have trouble with being away from her home or family but with getting used to being in God's presence. It made her nervous and scared, and she had almost never been scared before.

Slowly, very slowly, Amy began to trust. It started with one staff member, the night supervisor. For some reason Amy felt comfortable with her. Then she found another staff, the praise and worship leader, whom she trusted as well. She decided that they were the only two people she would trust. She had one during the day and one at night, and that was plenty.

Amy's fears kept her from communicating openly with the staff. The majority of her sharing was done in long letters written during her times alone. She did not feel that she was worth the time it would take to talk to her. Her choice to write out her feelings rather than talk about them was also based on the fact that if she just left a letter underneath the office door, she did not have to watch the person's reaction to what she had to say. That way she could avoid any possible rejection.

Several weeks into her stay, Amy began to feel just a little bit safe. That allowed her to be a little more open. She saw girls around her who had obviously changed. There were even people on staff who had once been in the program. Grudgingly she admitted that it might be possible for God to change someone's life. It was possible for them, that was, but not for her. She would never change.

That was a big step for Amy. She started to see that there was a chance for change. Her new outlook opened the door for the praise and worship leader to explain to her that change was only going to come when she let God in, and that He could not do anything in her life if she did not belong to Him. If Amy asked Jesus into her heart, He would come in and never leave her, according to Revelation 3:20 and Hebrews 13:5.

She told Amy that all she had to do was what is written in Romans 10:9 (NKJV), *if you confess with your mouth the Lord Jesus and believe in your heart that God has raised Him from the dead, you will be saved.* When asked if she was ready to do that, Amy surprised everyone, especially herself, by nodding her head. She asked God to come into her heart that day, and her name was written in the Book of Life (Philippians 4:3).

Accepting Christ did not solve all of Amy's problems. She still had years of pain, abuse, hurtful memories, and anger stored up inside of her. Constant thoughts of unworthiness and the fear of failure plagued her. Every time things started to get better, the old tapes of people telling her that she was not going to make it replayed themselves in her head.

It was obvious that Amy was growing. She was surrounded by the presence of God. For the first time, she decided that she wanted Him. Amy was most frustrated by not being able to feel God. Everyone told her that she would have to go by faith and the feelings would follow. That was very difficult for Amy, as trust was one of her biggest issues.

She continued to struggle with trust for quite some time. Although she had made progress by opening up to two of the staff, she knew she needed to go beyond that. Amy had just started to open up to her counselor when she left her position and moved on to something else that God had for her. It shocked Amy, and then it made her mad. The old fear of everyone she trusted being taken away from her resurfaced.

Amy was certain that she could not trust any of the other counselors. There was nothing wrong with them, but she had never felt a connection with them. The only daytime staff she could even imagine trusting besides the praise and worship leader was the program director, and she did not do any counseling. Amy believed that God had set her up to fail once again. She thought He was probably laughing at her stupidity.

The program director became Amy's interim counselor. The understanding was that all of the girls would be transitioned to a new counselor when one was hired. When that time came, the program director requested to keep Amy as a counselee. There was a true connection between them, and she believed God wanted her to continue counseling Amy.

When Amy discovered that her counselor would not be changing, she felt special to God for the first time in her life. Although she had never told anyone, the thought of switching counselors again had terrified her. God knew her need and He worked everything out, just as people had told her He would. Up until that point, she had firmly believed that He was against her. She began to understand Romans 8:31, *If God be for us, who can be against us?*

Amy was hungry for God's Word and she began to devour it. She no longer believed that the Bible was just a book but realized that it had relevance for her life. She wanted to learn all about it. Most of her counseling sessions were teaching sessions. She was not ready to verbally express much, and her counselor was patient with her. She understood that Amy knew so little of the truth about God that she needed time to cover the basics.

Her counselor provided her with lists of Scriptures about her identity in Christ, and she looked up every one of them. Amy also started her own list, writing down references to the Scriptures that impacted her in the front of her Bible so she could find them quickly. She began memorizing Scripture so that she could quickly call it to mind whenever she needed to combat the negative thoughts that continued to come.

The verse that encouraged her the most was Jeremiah 29:13 (NIV), *You will seek me and find me when you seek me with all your heart.* Amy wanted to find God and she believed she was making progress. Amy continued to struggle with not being able to feel God's presence, but that changed one night. God took an incident that Amy could have used as proof that everyone she trusted left her and turned it into proof that He would never forsake her.

The night supervisor whom Amy had trusted from the beginning came to her one afternoon to tell her that she was going to be switching to a daytime position. She would still be there every day, but Amy knew that it would not be the same. Immediately she began to blame God for taking away the one person at night she felt she could trust. She heard the staff member promise that God would bring in someone else Amy could trust, but she did not believe her. For the rest of the evening, Amy avoided her. She spent her time alone, crying out to God in anger.

Late that night, when everyone else had gone to bed, the staff member asked Amy to come into her office so she could talk to her. Amy finally opened up about how she was feeling. She cried—the first time in a very long time that she had cried in front of anyone. She expected to be told to get over it, to grow up. Instead, she was told that it was okay to be angry, and that God understood her feelings. For the next forty minutes, the staff member hugged Amy, cried with her, and prayed for her.

As Amy sat there and listened to the staff member pray for her, she suddenly felt as if someone had wrapped a warm blanket around her. She almost looked up to see who else was in the room when she realized that it was what she had been asking God to show her for so long. She was finally feeling His presence. It amazed her that after everything she had said to Him that day, He had still forgiven her and blessed her with the desire of her heart.

Finally, Amy was starting to believe that God might truly love her. There were still things that remained difficult for her. She did not understand why she had suffered abuse. Amy's counselor taught her that sometimes people are hurt as a result of the poor choices of others who are controlled by demons or fleshly desires. Scripture states in Ephesians 6:12 (NIV) that *our struggle is not against flesh and blood, but against the rulers, against the authorities, against the powers of this dark world and against the spiritual forces of evil in the heavenly realms.*

Amy finally understood this. While God uses those who have committed their lives to Him, Satan is free to use those who haven't made a commitment to Christ. She realized that she had been hurt by the bad choices of many people. While it was not easy, Amy was eventually able to forgive them and become free from much of the pain associated with the events.

Christmas break came and Amy spent two weeks at home. It was a hard time for her. Nothing had really changed, either with her parents or with Jana's family. Amy was learning that she did not have to depend on her natural family for acceptance because God had made her a part of His family according to 1 John 3:1. It was difficult for her to face the fact that she was unable to find the kind of love that she had always wanted from them and that they would probably never be able to provide that for her. She suffered several setbacks while she was home, doing things she had decided she would not do again, like drinking and watching horror movies.

When she returned to the program, Amy realized just how much those things had influenced her. She had never understood why Christians she knew were so against horror movies. After all, they were just make-believe. But, when depression and suicidal thoughts started hitting her again after all the victory she had achieved in those areas, she realized that she had opened a door to Satan.

Genesis 4:7 (NIV) says, ***sin is crouching at your door; it desires to have you, but you must master it.*** Amy clearly saw that she had allowed the devil to pounce right back into her life. Watching the horror movies reminded her of the days when she had been obsessed with death, and God had shown her new life. She had to choose life once again, according to Deuteronomy 30:19.

The next months were filled with ups and downs as Amy struggled to renew her mind according to God's Word. She believed that she had the mind of Christ, as it says in 1 Corinthians 2:16. Amy struggled to keep the mind of Christ. She had spent so much time thinking in the old patterns that it took time and effort to develop new patterns. She continued taking negative thoughts captive, making them obedient to Christ (2 Corinthians 10:5), and memorizing Scripture to replace them.

In addition to learning a new way to think, Amy also had to learn a new way to talk. Proverbs 18:21 tells us that the tongue has the power of life and death. Just as God spoke the world into creation, the words that we speak have creative power. In Job 22:28, God told Job that whatever he declared would be established. Job also said in Job 4:14 that the thing he feared came upon him. Positive or negative, the things we say often create the circumstances in which we live.

Amy had grown up with a negative mindset, consistently hearing putdowns and sarcasm. She had adopted that attitude for herself and much of the way she talked reflected it. The words "never" and "can't" were staples of her vocabulary. As she learned to trust God and walk by faith, not by sight (2 Corinthians 5:7), she also learned to speak in faith. She learned to ***call those things which do not exist as though they did,*** according to Romans 4:17 (NKJV). As she talked more positively, her life became more positive. She saw that she truly could do all things through Christ who strengthened her (Philippians 4:13).

It took over a year before Amy was ready to graduate. She believed that God was calling her to stay in the Nashville area. She wanted to get her life established away from her family and the old things that would threaten to drag her down again. I felt led to offer Amy a part-time position as a runner in the office, which she accepted. Over time, Amy proved herself faithful in the little things (Luke 19:7), and that part-time position turned into a full-time job. For a time, Amy served as my personal assistant and did a wonderful job helping me with the daily details of running the ministry.

Currently, Amy is working full-time as Residential Supervisor in our Nashville home. She is an amazing encouragement to the girls in the program. On a daily basis Amy is able to share what God has done in her life and be a living example of transformation! The girl who so desperately wanted to die is now sharing life and hope with others.

Things are not always easy for Amy. On a daily basis she has to put into practice the principles she learned while she was in the program. Sometimes she has learned the hard way, getting tripped up by one of Satan's snares. However, Proverbs 24:16 (NIV) says, *though a righteous man falls seven times, he rises again.* Amy has allowed God to pick her up each time and show her how to avoid the same trap in the future.

Each day, Amy's life is a representation of how God can make all things new. She has made a complete turnaround from an obsession with death to a determination to live and to fulfill the call God has on her life. She is always willing to give her testimony, knowing that God can use it to encourage others who have suffered some of the same things she did.

Amy's favorite verse is Psalm 118:17 (NIV), *I will not die but live, and will proclaim what the Lord has done.* Truly, He has done great things! Only God knows the details for sure, but He has definitely given her hope and a future (Jeremiah 29:11).

CHAPTER 13

WORKS IN PROGRESS

When a young woman enters Mercy Ministries, one of the first things she does with her counselor is set several goals she desires to achieve while in the program. As those goals are accomplished, the resident, her counselor, and the staff team evaluate her progress and begin to pray about a time for her to graduate. If the staff recognizes growth to the point where the young woman is showing evidence of a grounded and stable relationship with the Lord and beginning to reach out to help others, a graduation date is set.

Graduation is a special time at Mercy Ministries. Each graduate is presented with a ring that is specially made for her by a graduate who is now a jewelry designer. The ring serves as a physical reminder of the restoration that God has brought about in her life as a result of her obedience. It is also a symbol of the young woman's commitment to remain sexually pure until marriage.

During the ceremony, the graduate gives her testimony, relates how God changed her life. She also shares her hopes and dreams for her future. Often her family comes to share the day with her. The staff has the opportunity to gather around and pray for her as she prepares to leave as a new creation in Christ (2 Corinthians 5:17).

It was after one such graduation ceremony at the Nashville home that our receptionist told me a story I would like to share with you. I think it illustrates the transformation process that young women undergo when they come to Mercy Ministries seeking help.

A young woman who had graduated the program that morning was preparing to leave with her family. Her mother and sister beamed with pride, marveling at the difference in the girl whom they had left just a few months earlier. The love of Jesus radiated from her eyes and her beautiful smile glowed. As she was leaving, the other girls gathered at the balcony to see her off. She waved and blew kisses to them, grinning from ear to ear as she promised to keep in touch and always pray for them.

Just as she walked out one side of the front door, another young woman walked in the other side. She was just beginning her experience with God at Mercy Ministries. Her eyes never left the ground. Her shoulders were hunched over as if the weight of the world was heavy upon her. The smiles of her parents were forced, their faces etched with worry.

The difference between the two young women at that moment was striking. They were at opposite ends of the spectrum, one filled with excitement about the future God had planned for her and the other wondering if she even had a future. One walked in the assurance that she had a God who loves her, who had healed her wounds, and who would always be there for her. The other was desperate to discover whether what she had heard about a God who loved unconditionally was true because He was her last hope.

What amazed me so much about this story was not only the stark contrast of the two, but also the fact that the young woman who had been transformed and restored began the healing process in the same exact way as the hurting and broken girl. Her heart had been just as heavy and her future just as uncertain. God had met her needs in a unique and individual way, as He does with each young woman who submits herself to Him.

In the past sixteen years, over 2,000 hurting young women have come through the doors of the homes in Louisiana and Tennessee. Each one has been touched by the love of God and each life has been changed.

The healing is not instantaneous by any means, as many of the stories in this book illustrate. While in the program, the girls are a "work in progress." God seems to deal with them in layers, starting with the obvious things that need healing and then gently working down to the core of their issues. We call this "peeling the onion." It is often a difficult and painful process, but it is well worth it in the end. I want to share several stories of girls who are, as I write this, at different stages of allowing God to "peel" them.

CALLIE

Callie is the newest girl in the program, and she is one of our first international residents. She has suffered for years with an eating disorder that ravaged her body and left her hopeless. At seventeen years old, she stands at 5'5"and weighs just 85 pounds. Although she has a loving and committed Christian family, they were at a loss about how to help her fight this life-threatening battle. She had tried all the secular programs that were available in her home country; none of them were successful.

At the end of her rope, Callie cried out to God, asking Him to work something out for her that would bring her freedom. The only other option she had was to die. A series of events brought her thousands of miles away to Mercy Ministries. She was completely overwhelmed when she first arrived at the Nashville home. "Are you sure this is it?" she asked, staring at the building in front of her. She was so frightened by the magnitude of the problems she was facing in her life that she nearly fainted.

Now, just a few days after arriving, Callie says that God has already begun the restoration process. She is learning to be patient and give the timing of her life over to Him. Giving up control is a very frightening concept for Callie, but the staff and the other girls in the program are helping her see that God is worth trusting.

In spite of her fears, she is making progress. Her desire is to be secure and love herself, knowing who she is in Christ. She wants to be able to have a normal conversation over dinner without having to struggle through the constant battle in her head over what and how much she is eating. As she hears a steady stream of the Word of God and allows it to begin transforming her by the renewing of her mind (Romans 12:2), she is seeing small changes that keep her encouraged. She knows she is finally heading in the right direction.

Every day presents her with a new challenge. There seems to be so much that she has to work through that at times it appears to be too hard for one person to handle. Still, she has realized that Mercy Ministries is the right place to be in order to fight those daily battles. An environment that has supplied her with nothing but the love of God has given her the strength she needs to face the obstacles that meet her. She is learning the truth of God's Word that says His mercies are new every morning (Lamentations 3:23), and she is taking it one day at a time.

TAWANA

When Tawana came to Mercy Ministries, she was just fourteen years old and pregnant. Although she was scared, she never would have admitted to her fears at the time. She had learned early in life to be tough and hide her true emotions.

When she was two years old, Tawana was left with her aunt. Tawana's mother was strung out on drugs and living on the streets. She came in and out of Tawana's life, continually making and breaking promises to her. When Tawana was in the fourth grade, her mother came to get her and said she was taking her for good. Two weeks later, her mother sent her back to her aunt because she wanted to go out and party and Tawana was in the way.

Devastated, Tawana sank into a deep depression. She decided if her own mother could reject her, then everyone else would too. She slept for days at a time and refused to eat. By the time she was in the sixth grade, she was angry at everyone. Marijuana helped to ease the pain, as did alcohol, but nothing made her heart stop hurting.

Several members of Tawana's family were in a gang and she started hanging out with gang members and drug lords. She moved in with her mother and grandmother for three months when she was thirteen. Her mother did not care where she was, who she was with, or what time she came in, so Tawana did whatever she wanted.

After fighting with her grandmother and threatening her with a knife, Tawana was sent back to her aunt's home. She continued to hang out with the gang members without her aunt's knowledge and started seriously dating one. He was the only person in her life who listened to her and did not make fun of her when she cried. He simply handed her a tissue and a joint to ease the pain.

Tawana was a virgin and she was proud of that fact. When her boyfriend began pressuring her to have sex with him, she steadfastly refused. But one night, under the influence of both alcohol and drugs, Tawana gave in to his wishes. After that, there was no point in denying him. She eventually became pregnant by him.

Tawana had a hard time trusting God. She had heard that God was supposed to be a father. Her own father had never been there for her, so why should she trust God? Besides, He had never answered her prayers when she had cried herself to sleep every night praying for her mother to come home.

Tawana found herself with nowhere else to go. Her aunt had always been outspoken against teen pregnancy and Tawana knew she could not stay at her house. She did not want to be on the streets. Her boyfriend had been sent to jail, and although he promised that he loved her and would never leave her, there was not much he could do for her from behind bars. She heard about Mercy Ministries and reluctantly agreed to give it a try.

Tawana arrived with a chip on her shoulder. Her difficulty trusting God spilled over into an attitude with the staff that kept her busy with disciplines for most of her first month. Soon, however, it struck her that there was a baby coming and she did not know what she was going to do. For the first time in her life, she became serious. She dug into her counseling and began spending significant time in prayer.

Recently, Tawana made the decision to place her baby for adoption. Although it was very difficult for her to make this choice, she believes it is the best option for her and the baby. Every time she thought about parenting, she could not see anything in her future. When she thought about placing, however, she saw not only a better life for her child, but also high school graduation and college for herself.

As for her relationship with God, Tawana is working on that. She knows now that she loves God and wants Him to be a part of her life because without Him she was miserable. She also knows that He is the one true answer for hurting people. Her heart's desire is to become a psychiatrist. She says that rather than medicating patients, which does not help the heart, Tawana wants to be able to pray with them and help them see that only Jesus can meet their needs.

AMANDA

Amanda was in the ninth grade the first time she attempted suicide. The transition from a small junior high to a large high school was tough on her. She was depressed and felt she did not have any friends. A few months earlier, an acquaintance had raped her. No one understood her pain and she thought it would be easier to end it all.

Overdosing on pills brought her to a psychiatric hospital for a month. She did not find any answers there. Almost as soon as she got out, she overdosed again and went back for two weeks. That summer, Amanda tried to commit suicide for the third time and was placed in a state hospital because her parents' insurance money had run out. The doctors there prescribed medications for her but nothing helped.

The school put Amanda in a special program for the tenth grade, one in which she could be monitored at all times. She had been self-mutilating in class and done irrational things like tying her shoelaces around her neck to create a noose, or running out in the middle of traffic. Her behavior was becoming unmanageable.

Amanda's parents did not know what to do with her. They had always given her and her brother the best of everything and could not understand why this was happening. Doctors continued prescribing medications until Amanda was on sixteen different drugs at one time. They said that medicating her was the only hope.

At the end of the tenth grade, Amanda took herself off all her medications because she did not feel like they were helping her. She did well for a time, getting back into normal classes and making good grades at the beginning of the eleventh grade. The underlying issues had never been dealt with, however, and the depression returned.

When her grades began dropping again, Amanda became desperate. She had always wanted to be a doctor and knew she would never make it with her grades. Feelings of failure plagued her. Right before an appointment with her psychiatrist, she took a massive overdose. She collapsed in the waiting room and was rushed to the hospital in cardiac arrest.

Amanda was diagnosed with multiple personality disorder. The doctors at the psychiatric hospital told her parents to commit her to a state institution for life because there was nothing else they could do for her. They released her when there was no more insurance money. She had only been there a week.

Amanda begged her parents for one last try. It was a new school year and she believed she could go back with a clean slate and start over. They gave her another chance, but the stress and anxiety were too overwhelming. Within a few weeks she felt that she either had to go back to the hospital or she would kill herself. She chose to be readmitted.

Amanda's aunt is on staff at a church with which I have an excellent relationship, and I happened to be visiting when she went back to the hospital. Her aunt came to me and asked for my help, so I went to the psychiatric ward to see Amanda. Immediately I knew there was hope for her. She did not need drugs and institutionalization. She needed to know Jesus.

I spent some time talking with Amanda, telling her about Mercy Ministries and the confidence I had that she could find what she was seeking there. She was hesitant about having religion shoved down her throat, but I assured that we did not operate that way. She would be in a Christian environment and would be hearing all about God, but she would be allowed to make her own decisions.

One week later, Amanda came into the program. Within a few days, it became clear that many of her symptoms and disorders had been attention-getting and manipulative behavior. Her heart was hurting and she had never known how to express that in a healthy way. The suicide attempts and erratic behavior had all been cries for help.

The staff at Mercy Ministries made it virtually impossible for Amanda to manipulate. The more discipline she received for unacceptable behavior, the more Amanda realized that she was being forced to live within healthy boundaries because she was loved. It was the first time she had experienced true discipline. Once she realized that she would not be able to get her way like she was accustomed to with her family, Amanda began to settle down and honestly look at the issues of her heart.

Amanda is learning that the most important factor in her healing is her personal relationship with God. That is taking the place of all the other things she sought in her life to fill the emptiness or deaden the pain. Although the process has been difficult for Amanda, she is beginning to experience the stability that she has always desired.

JOANNA

Joanna's parents divorced when she was two years old. Her mother began dating another man within a year and he started molesting Joanna when she was four years old. He became her stepfather when she was five and began raping her when she was six. The sexual abuse continued until she was fourteen years old.

There was also a good deal of emotional and verbal abuse, as well as some physical abuse. In addition to all that she suffered at the hands of her stepfather, Joanna's brother began molesting her when she was seven. She tried to isolate herself as much as possible from her family, but they continued to inflict pain upon her.

Joanna closed herself off to all emotions except her anger, and most of that she turned inward. She often held her breath until she turned blue, and she repeatedly banged her head against the wall or rubbed her eyelids until they were raw. Even at a young age she hoped that if she hurt herself enough, someone would figure out something was wrong and ask her questions. She was too frightened to tell anyone on her own.

It was very difficult for Joanna to turn to God for help, even though she had been raised in church and had heard about Him most of her life. Her stepfather was very active at their church and her opinion of God was based mostly on what she saw in him. God, therefore, was not anyone she could trust.

The sexual abuse stopped when she was fourteen, but the guilt and shame continued. She slept in layers of clothes and did not shower for days. She wanted to do everything possible to make herself unattractive and protect herself from further abuse. The self-mutilation grew worse as she purposely tried to make herself ugly.

When Joanna was sixteen, her mother and stepfather divorced. It was an extremely confusing time for Joanna and she remained unable to sort out or express any of her emotions except anger. She turned her rage toward her mother, blaming her for breaking up the only kind of family that Joanna had ever known.

Alcohol eased some of the pain, but it never truly helped her. She eventually quit drinking but continued to live a numb life by shutting herself off from all emotions. She was functional, completing high school, attending college, and keeping a job. The whole time she continued to self-mutilate and constantly considered suicide. Only the fear of going to hell kept her from attempting it.

Joanna started seeing a counselor and many repressed memories of the abuse flooded to the surface. She was admitted to a psychiatric hospital, but it did not help. All of the other patients were in their 40s and 50s. As the youngest one in the ward, all Joanna could think was that her life was going to turn out just as theirs had. She felt like she was terminally ill because of the abuse and began to lose hope.

One thing Joanna did learn from her hospitalization was more ways to self-mutilate. By this time she was hurting herself up to six times a day, looking for some kind of release from the emotions that she kept trapped inside. She was so numb that the only time she knew she was a real person was when she cut herself and saw blood.

A suicide attempt forced her counselor to give her an ultimatum of going back to the hospital or trying a group home. The counselor knew about Mercy Ministries and offered to get her an application. Joanna had already started going back to church, knowing that God was the only possible answer. She was desperate for something to take away the pain. Believing that Mercy Ministries was her last hope, she agreed to come.

Although Joanna truly wanted to change, she was not expecting to have to dig through everything that she had worked so long to keep hidden. She wanted someone to say the magic words and make all the pain go away, but that was not what she found. For several weeks she considered giving up and going home, but she knew she would not find healing there.

After she made up her mind to stay and committed to working through her issues, Joanna began to see progress. She is learning how to trust God by giving Him areas of her life one by one. She has experienced how turning over painful memories to Him does not necessarily mean that they go away, but that the sting associated with them is gone. She is also learning to love God as her heavenly Father and to see that He would never hurt or abuse her.

Slowly, God is restoring Joanna's emotions to her. She had been so closed for so long that she thought anger was the only thing she would ever feel. Now she can sense the pain of others and is beginning to identify similar feelings within herself. Her counselor is helping her learn healthy ways to express those emotions.

When Joanna looks back at where she was less than a year ago, she is amazed by the change in herself. She knows now that she has a future—one that holds a promise for her. For the first time in her life, she is happy to be alive.

CHRIS

From the time Chris was a young girl she was confused about her identity and her purpose. Throughout her life she was abused by several different men and believed that there must be something wrong with her. She hated herself and spent most of her time wishing she was dead.

Chris had an understanding of God, but not of a relationship with Him. One of her abusers was a spiritual leader, a man she thought was supposed to represent God. That led her to have a distorted view of God. She came to a point where she thought He was evil and wicked, and she hated Him.

Her life spiraled downward quickly. Alcohol and drugs consumed her, helping her avoid the pain, or at least hide it enough to keep up a good facade. She covered up her turmoil by wearing many different fronts and masks, but on the inside she was tormented. At night she was plagued by severe nightmares.

Her hatred of herself was so intense that she began starving her body, trying to destroy who she was. Finally, at 27 years old, Chris came close to death. At a crucial moment, with 99% of her wanting to die and just 1% believing that there had to be something more, she cried out for help.

Chris began walking the streets of her Australian home city, knocking on the doors of rehabilitation centers and halfway houses, looking for anyone who would help her. She had no insurance, no money, and no time for a waiting list. No one took her in. Devastated, she went to a friend's house. Not entirely sure who she was talking too, she cried out one more time, "I'll do whatever it takes, go wherever I have to go. Just help me!"

God heard her cry. Twenty minutes later a friend called and offered to help her. As they began looking for places for her to go, they heard about Mercy Ministries. Chris sat down and wrote an e-mail explaining her situation as tears ran down her cheeks—the first time she had cried in years. Within two weeks, she was in the program.

It was an extremely hard decision for Chris to make, not only because she had to come so far, but also because she was not wholly convinced that there even was a God. Still, she had never felt peace like she did the moment she walked through the front doors of Mercy. Right then a voice, which she now knows belongs to God, promised her that He would finish what He had started (Philippians 1:6).

Chris has come a long way in the process of her healing. She understands now that God is a good God, and that He is there to help her, not hurt her. For the first time, she can say that she loves Him. He brought her from the very edge of hell to a place of hope.

It has been a difficult road for Chris. One of the hardest challenges has been forgiving the people who hurt her. It took her quite some time to decide to forgive them, but she finally understood that she was not doing it for them. It was between her and God. In order for that relationship to move ahead, she had to close the door to the past. Forgiveness is still an ongoing process for her, but it is one of the most freeing things Chris has ever done.

Recently, Chris went through an experience that proved to herself and everyone else how far she has come in the seven months she has been in the program. In the course of what we thought was a routine phone call to extend her visa, we discovered that the immigration officials had made an error and Chris's visa had actually expired six weeks earlier. She was, at that point, illegally in the country and had to return to Australia immediately.

Chris knew that God was not yet finished with the work He had begun in her. She made a decision to stand in faith and trust God that He would work out all the details for her speedy return. For a young woman who several months earlier could not fathom the concept of trusting God, that was a huge step.

When Chris returned to Australia and re-applied for her visa, it was granted to her within 45 minutes! It was truly a miracle. She was able to stay at home for about a week to visit with family and friends before returning. In addition, she even took advantage of the long plane flight to witness to another passenger! Only later did Chris learn that the passenger was the governor of the state of Tennessee.

As Chris approaches the end of her time in the program, she is beginning to see other girls whom she can encourage. She tries her best to comfort them with the same comfort she received from God, according to 2 Corinthians 1:3-4. It is her heart's desire to help others get through what she has been through. The people who have helped her the most are those who have been where she was and have spoken hope into her life. She believes that if God can use her to save just one life, the way He used Mercy Ministries to save hers, then all that she suffered will have been worth it.

HALEY

Haley describes her family as dysfunctional. Her mom was an alcoholic and her dad worked all of the time. They divorced when Haley was five years old. By the time she turned nine years old, her father had remarried. She lived with her dad and stepmother.

For her ninth grade year, Haley was sent to a boarding school. Missing her family and angry over her mother's absence from her life, Haley began to rebel. She got into fistfights with other girls at school and often disrespected her teachers. A fight with her dorm parents was the last straw and Haley was expelled.

Haley's parents put her into a psychiatric hospital in an attempt to figure out what was wrong with her. The insurance money ran out after a week and she came home without answers. She went to a public school, where she did not do much except sleep in class and start hanging out with the wrong crowd.

Although Haley's mother had been writing letters to her for several years, the anger that Haley held towards her caused her to refuse to read them. One night she decided she wanted to know what they said and asked her father for them. She sat in her room for several hours and read them all. Her mother wrote that she had stopped drinking and that if Haley ever wanted to come see her, she would be welcome.

When Haley finished reading the letters, she came out and announced to her father and stepmother that she wanted to live with her mom. They decided it might be a good idea. Haley packed her things and her dad and stepmom brought her to her mother's house without warning. Her mother rejoiced when she found out that her daughter wanted a relationship with her and welcomed her with open arms.

Haley began the tenth grade while living with her mother. She quickly found the same kind of friends she had in the last public school and got into the same kind of trouble. This group introduced her to drugs and she began to experiment.

The relationship between Haley and her mother was going well until one day Haley returned from a weekend with a friend to find her mother passed out on the couch. The refrigerator was stocked with beer. She had obviously relapsed. Although Haley had been young, she remembered what it was like living with an alcoholic mother and did not want to do it again.

Returning to boarding school was the only option that Haley's father and stepmother gave her. She felt like a toy that kept getting passed around and was never settled. She was hurt and angry with everyone, including God. She had asked Him not to take her mother away from her again, but it seemed He had not heard her prayer. Trust became impossible for her and depression set in. Her response was to rebel.

Within a week of her return to boarding school, Haley was caught smoking cigarettes and sniffing Ritalin. She was expelled again. She was sent to a halfway house but it was too expensive for her father to keep her there. He found out about Mercy Ministries and gave her the option of coming into the program or going to juvenile detention.

Haley chose to come to Mercy Ministries but did not truly have the desire to change. She had simply decided that it was a better option than juvenile detention. She thought she could play her way through the program to please her father and go back home. Quickly she discovered she would not be able to get away with that.

After a few weeks of playing games and several warnings from the staff about needing to get serious, Haley was called into the program director's office. She was told she was being sent home. It suddenly struck her that she was miserable and frustrated with her life and that her best opportunity to change was slipping through her fingers. If she were sent home, she would go to juvenile detention, where she knew she would not be taught about God and His plan for her life like she was being taught at Mercy. She cried and begged for another chance, which was given to her on the condition that she prove herself serious within a few days.

When Haley made her decision to get serious, she found that her life started to turn around. She began to deal with the rejection and the pain that her family circumstances had caused and she learned to look to God as her Father. In Psalm 27:10 God promises that although our earthly parents might forsake us, He will always receive us. Haley began to cling to that promise and discovered that God is faithful.

Mercy Ministries has become a family to Haley. It was the first place where Haley found people who loved her unconditionally and where the motivation for helping was not money. It was the place where she learned to put her trust in God and allow Him to heal the hurts in her life.

Haley has been in the program for over a year now. Although she is ready to graduate, there are still several circumstances that need to be settled. Her father has signed over his parental rights and given his permission for her to seek legal emancipation. She is pursuing her GED with the intention of going on to college.

With obvious talent in drama and the arts, Haley's desire to is to study dance and drama, as well as psychology. She wants to find a way to use her talents to communicate the life-changing message of God's love to teenagers who have experienced the same type of hurt and rejection that she did.

VICKI

When Vicki's family moved into a new neighborhood before she started the eighth grade, she quickly found herself an outcast. She did not care about clothes or money like the other kids her age who lived there. She found a few kids who thought like her and they spent their time drinking and smoking marijuana instead.

Vicki's grades started dropping and her parents knew there was something wrong. When she came home high on her sixteenth birthday, her parents took her to juvenile detention in an attempt to scare her straight. For two days Vicki pretended she did not care, but inside she desperately wanted someone to see how lonely she was.

Her parents took her to a counselor and she was put on anti-depressants. Although Vicki was depressed, what she needed more than medication was the attention and recognition of her parents. She was the middle child between her older brother and younger sister. They were all just one year apart. Rebellion was Vicki's attempt to define herself as her own person.

The depression worsened until Vicki was barely able to get out of bed. Drugs became her method of escape. She abused the prescription drugs that she was on, mixing them with other pills that her friends had. She also used acid, alcohol, and anything else she could find. Her need for the drugs controlled her and she did anything necessary to get them.

Vicki was sent to a psychiatric treatment center for two months. They monitored her medication and tried to find a better dosage, but could not help her. She returned to school and continued the drug abuse. One morning, she smoked marijuana before class and then accepted a Valium pill from a friend. The combination caused her to pass out and hit her head on the floor.

The fall fractured her skull. After treating the injury, the hospital admitted her to the psychiatric ward again. They told her she would be there for three days. When the three days became three weeks, Vicki was irate that they had lied to her. They could not handle her rage and she was transferred to a different center for a month. From there she went into a drug and alcohol rehab for another month and then to a halfway house.

Vicki ran away from the halfway house and, after a bad experience with being picked up by a car full of guys, called her parents. To her amazement, they came for her. It was a miracle that they were willing to give her another chance. They brought her home and enrolled her in an alternative school.

For a time she did well, but eventually the drug cravings became too strong. She took a handful of prescription drugs and her mother found the empty bottle in her room. It happened on a day she had a court date and when the judge was told about her continued drug abuse, he turned her over to the custody of the state.

The kids at the state facility fought all the time, and drugs were readily available. Vicki knew she was not in the right place. If she remained in state custody, she would be on her own when she turned eighteen. Although she was angry with her parents, she did not want to lose them. She realized that her behavior was destroying her relationship with her family and wanted to change. She needed to get real help.

Several months earlier, Vicki had heard about Mercy Ministries but decided against it. Now she saw it as the only chance she had to keep her family and she was ready. She submitted her application and was accepted. Immediately Vicki noticed the difference from the other programs she had tried. The staff truly cared about the girls, and she could tell that they were not just there for the money because they took the time to get to know her.

Just a few weeks into her stay at Mercy Ministries, Vicki asked Jesus into her heart during a counseling session. I will never forget hearing about how she announced her new life in Christ to the girls. During prayer time after the evening class, Vicki spoke up in her usual straightforward way.

"I got a praise report," she said. "Y'all don't have to worry about me. I ain't going to hell no more. I got saved today." The girls and staff rejoiced with her, welcoming her into the family of God with open arms.

Vicki decided to pursue her GED, knowing that going back to school and facing her old friends would be difficult for her. She spent several months studying and preparing for the test and recently passed it on the first try. We threw her a party to celebrate her achievement, complete with a cap and gown!

God has worked miracles in her family, fully restoring the relationships. Vicki no longer manipulates or lies to get her way with her parents and she takes responsibility for her choices rather than blaming them. The bitterness and anger she felt towards them were replaced with love when she opened her heart and let God heal the wounds those negative emotions were hiding.

After seven months in the program, Vicki is ready to graduate. Now that she understands that the need she was trying to meet by using drugs is only fully met in a relationship with God, she has no reason to return to her old habits. She is a true picture of 2 Corinthians 5:17 (NIV), which says, *Therefore, if anyone is in Christ, he is a new creation; the old has gone, and the new has come!*

ALLISON

Allison was adopted as a baby into a Christian family. Although she knew all the Bible stories, she did not have a personal relationship with Jesus. She describes herself as a "hyper kid who always wanted friends." From a young age she felt she always had to have a boyfriend. There was a void in her life from that she tried to fill with people. Unfortunately, those people often let her down.

Craving acceptance, Allison did whatever her friends were doing in order to fit in. She started drinking at fourteen years of age and was hooked on cocaine by the time she turned sixteen. Years of her life were spent in pursuit of the next high. Allison did whatever was necessary for the drugs or for the money to buy them, including stealing, dancing in nightclubs, and even prostituting herself.

Throughout her addiction, Allison believed that God was always with her. She prayed constantly and knows that He protected her through several suicide attempts and accidental overdoses. She met and married a man who believed in God as she did, but who also did not know how to take the head knowledge and make it a matter of the heart. Although they often prayed together for God to change them, they continued to choose drugs instead of the difficult path of getting clean.

Allison went in and out of jail and secular treatment programs for her addiction, but never found any answers. Programs that told her she would always be an addict and in recovery only gave her an excuse to continue the behavior. She believed that her identity was wrapped up in being an addict for the rest of her life and felt hopeless.

When Allison was arrested for writing bad checks and found herself in jail once again, it finally hit her that she needed to change. She hated her life and was going nowhere. Her husband was also in jail, and there was nothing he could do to help her since his addiction was equally life-controlling.

Allison's mother brought her information about two places that she thought might be options for help, and Allison chose to come to Mercy Ministries. She knew that God was going to be her only answer and could only hope that she would find something at this program that was different from the others she had tried.

From the beginning Allison knew that this was what she had been searching for her whole life. For the first time, she was taught that her identity was in Christ and not in a label such as "alcoholic" or "drug addict." She heard testimonies of people who had been totally set free from their addictions, and she knew that was what she wanted.

As Allison learned more and more about God and His incredible love for her, she began to turn to Him for acceptance rather than seeking it from the people around her. She understood that He would be able to meet all of her needs, just as His Word promises in Philippians 4:19. Within a few short weeks of entering the program she was completely set free from the need for drugs and alcohol.

With that behind her, Allison focused on her relationship with God. She began asking Him to heal the damage that had been done to her family. At the time she entered the program, her father could barely speak to her, much less tell her that he loved her. The memories of the times Allison had told him that she hated him and the pain she had caused the family were still too fresh in his mind. Little by little, God drew them closer together, until now the relationship has been completely restored.

Other miracles happened in Allison's life as well. All the charges against her were dropped as a result of seeking help at Mercy Ministries. Financial concerns were completely covered by family and friends, and Allison will be able to attend college in the fall to study social work and English. In addition, she was totally healed from a serious physical illness!

Any time the desire to drink or do drugs tries to tempt her, she simply plays the whole scene out in her mind, remembering the pain and destruction that it caused in her life before. She knows for certain now that a momentary high is nowhere near worth the agony. She also relies on the "four stay-ins" that the girls are taught as they prepare to leave the program—stay in church, stay in prayer, stay in the Word, and stay in fellowship with other believers. She knows that those things will keep her strong as she walks in the freedom she has received.

Allison has been like a sponge throughout her four months in the program, soaking up everything that she could possibly learn. Even she is amazed by the change in herself. Now when she thinks about her future, she gets excited by the hope and potential she sees. She knows without a doubt that God has set her feet firmly upon the rock and that He will be there every time she reaches out to keep her from slipping.

Each one of these remarkable young women is at a different stage in her process of healing, or "peeling." Every one of them has learned that as they take a step of faith that God calls them to take, He is faithful to meet them where they are. He has promised to complete the work He has started in them and He will continue to do so, long after they graduate and leave Mercy Ministries.

Because there is a continuous stream of new girls coming into the program, as well as girls completing the program, there will always be "works in progress." It is my heartfelt desire that at whatever point you may read this book, you will lift up a prayer for all those young girls who are presently "works in progress." *Remember, today's challenges are tomorrow's testimonies.*

CHAPTER 14

WHERE DO WE GO FROM HERE?

Where do we go from here? I can't say that I have one definitive answer for that question. Mercy Ministries is experiencing an exciting time of growth at a pace that I have never before experienced. Sometimes it seems things are happening so fast that I can't keep up!

In 2000, we accepted girls into our first international home in Sydney, Australia. Mercy Ministries in flourishing and growing in that nation, and a second home has been opened in Queensland! The plan is that there will be a home in each of the seven states of Australia.

We have also established our national headquarters in Nashville, Tennessee, which keeps the current homes functioning and is the center of all future planning for the ministry's expansion. Moving into this corporate office building doubled the capacity of the Nashville home and allowed us to minister to more girls in need.

Joyce Meyer, my friend and a longtime financial supporter of Mercy Ministries, and her husband, Dave, felt led to help start a Mercy Ministries home in St. Louis and have donated property there to establish a home. We are currently in the process of renovating that facility. Opening the home in St. Louis will relieve some of the pressure on the waiting list, but not for long. The calls for help increase every day, and there is much more to be done.

Fortunately, our God knows what we have need of before we even ask! Relationships have been established and plans are underway for future homes in Seattle, Washington, Houston, Texas, Los Angeles, California and Oklahoma City, Oklahoma. We also have an office in the United Kingdom and staff working on opening a facility there, and have launched Mercy New Zealand in that nation as well.

The vision of Mercy Ministries continues to spread throughout this nation and others, growing and expanding as God directs and provides. There are so many things God has placed in my heart about the future of this ministry that it is difficult to share them in a few short pages. I ask you to keep us in prayer as we seek God's face and His will for the direction of this ministry in the coming days, months, and years. There are many challenges that confront us on a daily basis, but I know that God's grace is sufficient in our weakness.

God reminded me not long ago that *today's challenges are tomorrow's testimonies.* Thank you for your partnership with us as we continue to see precious young women come through the doors of our program and receive the help that they so desperately need. It is so exciting to watch those testimonies unfold on a daily basis. I look forward to sharing more and more of their stories with you as mercy *continues* to move mountains!

PRAYER OF SALVATION

God loves you—no matter who you are, no matter what your past. God loves you so much that He gave His one and only begotten Son for you. The Bible tells us that "...whoever believes in him shall not perish but have eternal life" (John 3:16 NIV). Jesus laid down His life and rose again so that we could spend eternity with Him in heaven and experience His absolute best on earth. If you would like to receive Jesus into your life, say the following prayer out loud and mean it from your heart.

Heavenly Father, I come to You admitting that I am a sinner. Right now, I choose to turn away from sin, and I ask You to cleanse me of all unrighteousness. I believe that Your Son, Jesus, died on the cross to take away my sins. I also believe that He rose again from the dead so that I might be forgiven of my sins and made righteous through faith in Him. I call upon the name of Jesus Christ to be the Savior and Lord of my life. Jesus, I choose to follow You and ask that You fill me with the power of the Holy Spirit. I declare that right now I am a child of God. I am free from sin and full of the righteousness of God. I am saved in Jesus' name. Amen.

If you prayed this prayer to receive Jesus Christ as your Savior for the first time, please contact us on the web at www.harrisonhouse.com to receive a free book.

Or you may write to us at
Harrison House
P.O. Box 35035
Tulsa, Oklahoma 74153

ABOUT THE AUTHOR

Nancy Alcorn, president and founder of Mercy Ministries of America, spent the first eight years of her career working with teen juveniles and then investigating child abuse cases. It was during this period that Nancy realized the inadequacy of these programs to offer real transformation in the lives of troubled young women.

Nancy knew that only Jesus could bring restoration into the lives of these girls who were so desperately hurting, and she knew that God was calling her to step out and do something about it.

In 1983, she founded Mercy Ministries of America, a residential facility for troubled girls ages 13-28. Presently, Mercy Ministries operates homes and licensed adoption agencies in various cities around the world. Plans are underway to open additional homes in the United States and in other countries.

Check out our website at **www.mercyministries.com** to find out more information about **Mercy Ministries of America** and information regarding the following:

- How to become a financial donor
- To obtain an application for admission
- For national and international locations of Mercy Ministries' homes
- To receive information about our adoption services
- To receive quarterly newsletter
- To purchase product resources

Mercy Ministries of America asks that you please contact our National Headquarters in Nashville, Tennessee, for additional information regarding the following:

- Speaking Engagements
- Employment Opportunities
- Volunteer Opportunities
- All Other Inquiries

Mercy Ministries of America

P.O. Box 111060
Nashville, TN 37222-1060
Phone: (615)831-6987
Fax: (615)315-9749
Email: info@mercyministries.com
Website: www.mercyministries.com